GW00646758

Graham

Glimpses of Faith

Glimpses of Faith

One hundred meditations for today

by

GEORGE APPLETON

Formerly Archbishop in Jerusalem

MOWBRAY

LONDON & OXFORD

ISBN 0 264 66788 3

First published in this collection 1982
by A.R. Mowbray & Co. Ltd.,
Saint Thomas House, Becket Street,
Oxford, OX1 1SJ

This material first appeared in the *Daily Telegraph* Saturday Meditation, and is reprinted with permission.

Typeset by Coats Dataprint Ltd.,
Smithton Industrial Estate, Smithton,
Inverness, Scotland

Printed in Great Britain by
Richard Clay (The Chaucer Press) Ltd.,
Bungay, Suffolk

Contents

PART FOUR: Towards Maturity

PART FIVE: Towards Eternity

Preface

I am very grateful to the *Daily Telegraph* for inviting me to take a share in its Saturday meditations, grateful for the trust and freedom its editors have given me, and grateful for permission to publish in book form 100 of those meditations.

To follow Dean Walter Matthews is an honour to one who knew him and loved him, who admired him for his depth of thought, his wide interests, his frank honesty and his humility. The then Editor was very wise and urged me not to try and imitate Walter Mathews, but to be myself and speak from my own heart and experience.

The present Editor, Mr Walter Deedes, urged me not to be ephemeral and topical, but to concentrate on the eternal verities, a piece of advice I was only too pleased to try and follow.

The task of writing these weekly meditations was shared with Dean Michael Stancliffe, alternating three months at a time. This accident of calendar and division of labour has meant that, as we have kept roughly to the same period each year, in this present selection of my meditations there is much more about the death of Jesus and the conviction that he is the ever-living one and the ever-present one, and little mention is made of his birth.

To say something of value, complete in itself in 350 words (when one's own natural length seems to be more like 500 words), was not easy. The need for compression demanded that every unnecessary word and every tangential thought, however seemingly valuable, had to be discarded.

I have also to express my gratitude to the many readers who have written to me during the past 7 years. Some expected a complete manual of faith and theology in every meditation. Some felt that I was a lost soul, destined for the fires of hell. Many wanted further elucidation, and quite a number wanted comfort and a spiritual confidante. I am grateful to all who have written and have answered most letters. Their comments showed me the gaps in my thinking and suggested further subjects for meditation.

In a series of meditations over a period of seven years, there is bound to be some repetition of themes, thoughts and even quotations. If these are of any value or depth, they can well be repeated, representing the insights which appeal to me most, the values by which I try to live, and of which I need constant reminder. Yet this makes clear that the meditations are meant to be read and studied individually, and not read through continuously. This aspect comes out more clearly when it is remembered that the meditations appeared at weekly intervals, and were followed every week by a week-end of leisure, with time for consideration of the deeper issues of life.

I have no idea of how many readers study these short meditations, but I am sure that they form a much larger congregation than gather in church every succeeding Sunday when I happen to be the preacher, even though vicars and congregations make a special effort when a bishop is preaching.

I am also grateful to the publishers of these meditations, Mowbray's, who asked if they might make a selection of them available in a more permanent form.

Finally, I would thank Mrs Diana Hanmer, who does the weekly typing, and feels a responsibility for the relevance and quality of each meditation, as well as ensuring that it reaches the Daily Telegraph in time for inclusion in its weekly pulpit.

Easter 1981 G.A.

PART ONE

Towards Faith

1 First all the way

The first of the Ten Commandments 'Thou shalt have none other gods but me', governs all the rest. Later its implications were worked out in what Jesus, like some contemporary rabbis, designated as the first and greatest commandment of the Torah, the Law of the Lord: You shall love the Lord your God with all your heart, and with all your soul, and with all your mind and with all your strength (Mark 12.30). This says to me that I must love God with all my being, with all my mind and will, for the whole of my life. Totally!

God is to be the central fact, the first priority, the ultimate reality, the supreme loyalty, the greatest value, the decisive factor in the planning of my life. It is clear that this was so in the case of Jesus. It should be equally so in the life of every believer in God. If it were so, even in a sizeable minority of believers, the world would be a different place, closer to the Law of the Lord and the Kingdom of God, God's rule in the hearts and in the affairs of men.

I need to examine myself searchingly and critically to discover if this is so. Do I put God first in everything? Or do I put something else in that first place — my career, success, reputation, worldly honour, some loved one? Money? In the secret place of my heart, what do I value most, what do I work for, what in the last resort would I be ready to die for?

Are there other gods which usurp this total demand — family, class, political ideology, nationalism, religious denominationalism? If I put God first in everything all other loyalties will take their proper place, I shall serve them better through him.

A verse from the Psalms expresses what I am trying to say, 'Thou art my God, my goods are nothing unto thee', or as one modern translator puts it 'I have no good beyond thee', while another words it 'My welfare rests in thee alone'. God alone! Then I am safe, and can take my part in creating the world that God wants.

2 Treasure hunt

I have always been fascinated by two Biblical experiences which seem to say something significant about God. The first is the experience of Moses at the Burning Bush, where he hears an inner voice directing him to go back to Egypt to liberate his people. In response, he asks the name of God which will authenticate his mission and command a hearing. He is told in effect 'All that you can say of me is *"I AM"*.' God is eternal being in himself and the ground of being in man. You cannot reduce him to one name. He is nameless and can therefore be spoken of by a thousand names. No one name can identify him, or exhaust his meaning. By whatever name we call him, he will answer, and in the resulting meeting we shall come to know him as one who speaks, who answers and makes himself known.

The second fascinating experience is that of Paul at Athens, where looking round that centre of human wisdom he came across an altar with an inscription which has been variously translated: 'To an Unknown God', 'To the Unknown God', 'To God the Unknown', while some scholars suggest 'To God the Unknowable', with the clue that he is undiscoverable by human thinking, though this may start us off on an adventurous journey of discovery. God is the great eternal mystery, who can only be truly known by what he reveals of himself.

An early English mystical writer says that God cannot be grasped by thought, but only by love. If God is love in his essential being, and if we are made in his likeness we can get to know him by love. A further way is provided by prayer but only if we give equal value to silence and listening as we do to thought and speaking. Each of us needs a burning bush, and an altar on which to inscribe our faith.

3 Truth has many facets

The oath which a person takes in court to speak the truth, the whole truth, and nothing but the truth, is a direct consequence of the original ninth commandment to bear no false witness against one's neighbour. Those who framed it and we who sometimes take it know from our inner life as well as from experience of others how easy it is to leave out something or add something which will either excuse our action under review, present us in a better light or put the blame on others.

Jesus in interpreting the original Commandment to his followers urged them to speak the plain unvarnished truth — let your 'yes' be yes, and your 'no' be no, anything further is likely to distort the truth. He also insisted on the demand for truth whether on oath or not, so the truth, the whole truth, the truth always.

I can see the temptations to myself to defect from the truth, and the more I am aware of this human tendency the more I seem able to recognise exaggeration in advertisements, attempts in public relations to cover up the truth or polish up the image of the speaker. In court it is easy and tempting to present a plausible story about a trembling figure in the dock or the witness box, while in the media there must often be a strong impulse to heighten the sensational value or choose an eye-catching headline.

One of the psalmists says that God requires truth in the inward parts, and one of our most treasured prayers used as preparation for every service of Communion says that to him all hearts are open, all desires known and no secrets are hid. Christians believe that the truth was personified in Jesus Christ, Buddhists believe the same of the Buddha and people of other faiths and religions will have their own standard in person or teaching.

Believers in God would say that he is ultimate truth, and agree that the closer we come to him in prayer and meditation the greater the hope that we shall become silicon chips of the eternal truth.

I have amassed a disconcerting number of facets of truth — the whole truth, nothing but the truth, the truth always, truth in thinking and speaking, truth before God and truth in the depth of my being. Given all this I can leave my image to take care of itself.

4 Top of the pops

Joseph of Nazereth must have been a very good father. For Jesus, even as a boy of twelve, when he wanted to picture God, thought of him as Father, and later when he wanted to share his knowledge with other prople, used the same universal analogy. He took the thought of his people and religion daringly further by using the familiar family name 'Abba' which can most nearly be translated 'Dad' or even 'Pop'.

Once when I was flying to Jerusalem a boy in the back of the plane wanted to attract the attention of his father sitting in the front, and called out 'Abba! Abba!' The father immediately stood up, and my heart warmed to the boy, his father and to Jesus who used the same call to God.

Jesus spoke of God as if he knew him intimately, not just a knowledge *about* God, which biblical scholars, theologians, clergy, religious ideologists, even critics and atheists claim to have. He spoke of God as caring for each of us individually as well as in the mass, calling each one of us by name, responding to our 'Abba, dear Father' with his 'My child, my very dear child', an almost unbelievable intimacy.

Yet Jesus never ceased to remind us that God is '*Our* Father', father of us all, so that we are brothers and sisters to one another and to him. At every step he turned to the Father for supporting love and guidance: 'Father, I thank you', 'Father, your will be done', 'Father, if it be possible!', 'Father, forgive them', 'Father, into your hands'. Using the word 'you' sometimes is the nearest I can get to the audacity of 'Dad'.

What about people whose experience of a human father is so tragic that the word is no comfort or inspiration? Perhaps 'Mother' could be more meaningful, though psychologists tell us that many of their patients need 'a father figure'. We may have to find a satisfactory analogy of our own. It could be divine, psychologist, social worker, doctor, teacher, nurse, probation officer, prison warder, perhaps 'father' in a trade union chapel, or even bishop!

5 The best of both

I have often longed for a pronoun which would cover both 'he' and 'she'. This wish is now being strengthened by the discussion about the role of men and women in religion.

Western religious societies on the whole have been patriarchal in their thinking about God. The great majority of Jews, Christians and Muslims think of God as exclusively male, but all down Christian history there have been occasional scholars and saints who have thought otherwise. Anselm circa (1100 AD) prays:

But you, too, good Jesus, are you not also a mother? Is not he a mother, who like a hen gathers his chicks beneath his wings? Truly, Lord, you are a mother too!

Julian of Norwich in one day in 1373 received sixteen showings of divine love, and insists on referring to God as Mother. She prays 'My kind Mother, my gracious Mother, my beloved Mother, have mercy upon us'. To her fatherhood means power and goodness; motherhood means wisdom and lovingness. She does not develop the idea of divine feminity as opposed to that of masculinity, but includes both in her conception of the totality of God. The motherhood of God is complementary to his fatherhood.

Julian also speaks of 'my precious Mother Christ', which includes not his authority only, but his tenderness and supporting love. She quotes St John's text 'Whoever is born of God does not sin', and adds that the phrase 'to be born of' refers properly to the mother.

There are Bible texts which present a motherly image, e.g. Isaiah 49.15: 'Can a woman forget her sucking child, that she should have no compassion on the son of her womb? Even these may forget, yet I will not forget you.' Hosea pictures God as holding Israel in his arms and teaching them to walk. Jesus weeps over Jerusalem and the world in loving compassion. Clearly God combines the protectiveness of the Father with the tenderness of the Mother. We are discovering more of the allness of God and more of our own deep selves, made in the likeness of the Creator.

6 Crazy!?

Some of the parables of Jesus take a good deal of thought before you discover the real point. Take for example the story of the casual labourers in the vineyard. The owner went out at various times during the day to take on workers waiting to be employed, promising to pay each whatever was right. At the end of the day he insisted on paying the latest to be hired first and going on to pay the same daily wage to all, regardless of how many hours they had worked. Not surprisingly there was considerable grumbling on the part of those who had worked all day. The point of the parable is that if you insist on thinking of God as an employer this is the kind of thing you will find him doing.

He is like an employer who welcomes his servants back from their work on the farm, makes them sit down and waits on them.

He tells his followers that if they are compelled by authority to undertake a public duty for a mile and are then paid and discharged, they should be prepared to go a second mile without payment.

He does not expect the same profitability but he rewards those who make good use of whatever is entrusted to them. All are invited to enter equally into the master's joy.

You are expected to return good for evil, love for hatred. Anyone who comes for help must be given some kind of help.

He will count any good done to the least of his children as if it were done to himself. Fair enough! But he goes on to say that he will count refusal to come to the rescue of his needy ones as deliberate refusal to minister to him. And this judgement is applied to nations as well as individuals.

It all bears out a word of God heard by Isaiah, 'For my thoughts are not your thoughts, neither are my ways your ways. . . . For as the heavens are higher than the Earth, so are my ways higher than your ways, and my thoughts than your thoughts'. I thank God that this is so.

7 Interpreting experience

The first Christians were all Jews, believing firmly in the unity of God. They experienced God as creator. When they met Jesus their first impression was of an inspiring teacher and prophet who spoke of God in an authentic and convincing way. They hoped that he was the expected Messiah. With his death, their faith was shaken, but with the surprising experience that he was still living they came to believe he was in some way divine. As they moved out to the world, they experienced a spiritual presence always with them to guide and strengthen. so they experienced God as creator, incarnated in Jesus and ever present in the Holy Spirit. How could they interpret this three-fold experience?

The word 'Trinity' does not occur in the New Testament. Later Christians coined it to express the three-fold relationship they, like the original twelve, experienced. I sometimes feel bothered by the arithmetical analogy 'Three in one and one in three', yet I welcome the thought of the supra-personality of God, speaking of an eternal sufficiency and an inner relationship of love.

Christians have always tried to find analogies for this three-fold relationship and experience. Sunday school teachers used to talk of the clover leaf, but its three components seemed too distinct. Others spoke of the spring, the stream and the river. If, as the Bible believes, man is made in the image of God then perhaps thought, feeling and will, all three in the unity of the one personality, offer the most satisfying model, particularly as we do not think of the three 'persons' as operating independently.

We dare not claim to fathom the mystery of the divine Being, though we may perennially wonder at our experience of him as Father, Son and Holy Spirit. Many perhaps are content to take the undefined relationship in the the Apostle' Creed and to pray gratefully with St Paul:

'The grace of our Lord Jesus Christ, and the love of God and the fellowship of the Holy Spirit be with you all evermore'. That gem of spirituality demands some quiet contemplation.

8 Making images

Meditating on the Bible's prohibition of images, my memory recalls the story of an army chaplain who had preached a powerful sermon on the Ten Commandments. After the service he saw one man sitting with his elbows on his knees and his hands over his face, the picture of dejection. Going to enquire what was the matter he heard him mutter 'Well, I haven't made a graven image . . . at any rate not yet!'.

No graven image is worthy of the Living God, the Eternal Spirit, the source of holiness, perfection and love. Nowadays few of us would make a metal image, but many of us make a mental image and are tempted to think that we know all about God, that we have got him taped in our theological picture of him.

In the quiet contemplative prayer which so many people are feeling for today, our minds are stilled, conceptual thinking and mental images disappear, our whole attention is concentrated on God himself. Our minds are empty of everything except God, alert, waiting, silent and expectant.

This implies that God comes to us, that he takes the initiative, he speaks. I have to be still, my whole being open to him, my talkative inner voice silent, so that I can hear the still small voice within.

Yet most of us need some mental picture of God, and this has been given to us in Jesus Christ. Paul speaks of Jesus as the image of the invisible God, the writer of Hebrews says the same and John says that no one has ever seen God; the Son who is in the Father's heart has made him known. A modern Biblical scholar speaks of Jesus as 'the human face of God'.

Even then, our understanding of Jesus needs to be purified and perfected. Our mental picture of him, our present image of the Father has constantly to be changing as we come into closer touch with him, learn from the lives of saintly people and from the collective experience of the Church down the ages, until finally with the saints and servants of God we come to see his face.

9 A sound of gentle stillness

Halfway between Jerusalem and Bethlehem is a monastery dedicated to St Elijah. It is built on the site where Elijah is said to have rested in his flight to the desert to escape the revenge of the heathen queen whose priests he had discredited. Dispirited and exhausted, he lies down to sleep under a juniper bush. In a dream he sees a cruse of water and some bread baked on a small fire, and hears a voice urging him 'Arise and eat, else the journey will be too great for you'. Elijah does so and is strengthened for his journey down to the desert where Moses had been conscious of the divine presence.

Arrived at the mount of God, he experiences in succession a great storm which brings the rocks tumbling down the mountainside, and then an earthquake which shakes the whole mountain, and finally a fire which runs along the desert scrub. None of these happenings move him. The Bible record continues 'and after the fire a still small voice'. The prophet wraps his face in his mantle, realising that he is in the presence of God, called to account for his flight and finally sent back to continue his prophetic task.

One has to listen in silence to hear that voice and understand what it is saying. If man has a spark of the divine within him, as I believe, it is reasonable to hope for some inner communication. But one has to be quiet, and thought stilled, to attend and to listen. This has become more and more difficult in our noisy world.

In one of the early manuscripts the phrase 'a still small voice' is translated as 'a sound of gentle stillness' which suggests a gentle breeze rustling through a field of summer corn, giving a sense of peace and lack of hurry. In that silent stillness the deep self can speak or the voice of conscience come to the surface or the Spirit of God whisper in the language of the heart.

Elijah's experience in his hurried flight to the desert can be ours also: 'Arise and eat, else the journey will be too great for you'. Nourishment for the spirit is needed and is available — in sacrament and in every touch with the God who speaks so quietly, so gently, so persistently.

10 Kiss of life

Elisha was a gentle prophet compared to his fiercely righteous predecessor Elijah. A farmer's wife had said of him 'I perceive that this is a holy man of God who is constantly passing our way', a tribute that many of us clergy would like to be paid. Faced by the farmer's wife in her bitter grief at the death of her son, he had gently chided his critical servant 'Let her alone, for she is in bitter distress; and the Lord has hidden it from me, and has not told me', a gentleness that has often reproved me when I have wanted to retort angrily to some critical or angry attack. A little later he had been the first known person to use the kiss of life, to the apparently dead child of the farmer and his wife.

He had healed a Syrian general who had come to him on the advice of a little slave girl captured from Israel. He had more than once saved his own king from military disaster by wise knowledge and advice. On one occasion a Syrian detachment had been sent to surround and capture him. In reply to the despairing remark of his personal attendant he had said 'Fear not, for those who are with us are more than those who are with them', and the young man's eyes had been opened to see an army of chariots of fire around his master.

We today need to see behind the phenomenal and physical into the spiritual and eternal, where the forces of God are always alert to guard the true and the eternal and to strive for the righteous loving will of God. A New Testament writer had the same sense of spiritual insight when he said of Moses 'He endured as seeing Him who is invisible.' He went on to picture a great cloud of witnesses, rather like the crowd at some Olympic Games cheering on their particular athletes, anxious for all of us to achieve our best so far.

So putting myself under Elisha as a guru or teacher, I learn the need of gentleness and the value of spiritual eyesight. Elisha when his master Elijah had been about to be taken from him had asked for a double portion of his spirit as a legacy. I would be glad of a double portion of Elisha's spirit as well, so that strength can be tempered with gentleness, as I believe quiet confident strength always is.

11 Not this! Not this!

Sometimes in our desire and search for God we are helped by thinking of what he is not. Seekers in India have emphasised this negative way, and through the centuries there have been Christian thinkers and mystics who have commended it. T.S. Eliot experienced it: 'In order to arrive at what you do not know, you must go by a way which is the way of ignorance. In order to possess what you do not possess, you must go by the way of dispossession.' And he acted on his own advice: 'I said to my soul, be still, and let the dark come upon you, which shall be the darkness of God.' We need to be very humble, very still and receptive, trusting that out of the silence a voice will speak, and in the darkness we shall be given a new kind of sight.

One of the assumptions we reject in this negative approach is that God is the cold, passionless, unmoving, unchanging absolute of some philosophers. God does not change in his essential and eternal Being, his will is unalterably for truth, rightness and love, yet his wisdom shows us how to adapt to changing knowledge and conditions. I cannot for a moment accept that he is unfeeling, that he does not suffer in the sufferings of humans into whose patient creating he has put something of himself. Nor can I believe that he does not grieve in the recalcitrance of most of us and in the painfully slow progress towards the maturity and happiness of his plan. It has been said that there was a cross in the heart of God, before there was ever one on Calvary.

The Bible constantly speaks of compassion as one of the attributes of God; compassion is exemplified in the life of Jesus; every chapter of the Qur'an opens with the words, 'In the name of Allah the compassionate'. To suffer with, to identify ourselves with, is an ingredient implanted by God in human nature. To exercise compassion in feeling and action is to be god-like. A few minutes of quiet will reveal whether we have it or not.

12 All change here!

'What has been is what will be, and what has been done is what will be done; and there is nothing new under the sun'. This seemingly pessimistic interpretation of human life comes from a book of the Bible. Re-reading that book I have the impression that the writer was describing life without God.

The prophet Isaiah saw God always at work in world affairs: 'Behold, the former things have come to pass, and new things I now declare; before they spring forth I tell you of them'. Jesus promised that the Spirit would show his followers things to come, and the disciple closest to his mind heard the glorified Christ declare 'Behold! I am making all things new'.

Clearly, believers in God cannot agree that God is the sanctifier of the status quo, nor can we acquiesce in the idea that everything that happens is for the best. If our present world is the best possible, I should despair not only of man but of God. Contrariwise, I believe that God is always at work to complete the universe he is creating. We have not got it yet, but there is hope and assurance. The promise of the prophets is that one day the earth shall be filled with the knowledge of God as the waters cover the sea.

St Paul gives us a double clue when he says that the whole creation is groaning in travail, that is in the birth pangs of a new order, and he adds that creation is waiting for the supporters of God to stand up and be counted.

God does not change in his eternal being, but he is always working for change in the hearts and behaviour of people and in the human society in which we live. His will is to transform the world with all its tragedy and recalcitrance into his kingdom of righteousness, love and happiness.

An American church historian has given us the following prayer:

God grant me the serenity to accept the things I cannot change, the courage to change the things I can, and the wisdom to know the difference.

I want to add another clause to this lovely prayer:

and help me to discover what he wants done in the baffling changes of individual life and human society.

13 God-shaped hollows

Jesus was a very welcome guest at a home in Bethany on the outskirts of Jerusalem, where a brother and two sisters lived their quiet lives, and from time to time provided quiet refreshment for him, particularly as tension and danger mounted. The two sisters were very different people: the elder a practical, bustling, managing kind of person, more concerned with the meal than the guest, and the younger a quieter, more reflective type, eager to talk to the guest and listen to him.

We need something of both in our make-up, if we are to find peace of heart and right relationships with others. We need time to reflect, understand the meaning of life, interpret the signs of the times and find guidance about what we should and can do, and also assurance of hidden sources of strength.

It is an amazing thing that in a period of rapid change when the familiar landmarks seem to have disappeared, a time of frustration and seeming meaninglessness, of near anarchy and violence, there should be observable in all religions a desire for a deeper inner life and a growing conviction that it is in the spirit of man that the main battle is to be fought. A great novelist, usually regarded as hostile to religion, spoke of a God-shaped hollow in the heart of man. Augustine in the fourth century, at a similar period of change and disintegration diagnosed the same need: 'Thou has made us for thyself and our hearts shall find no rest until they find their rest in thee.'

Anselm, Archbishop of Canterbury around the year AD 1100 said something similar:

Come now, little man [he is talking to himself], put aside your business for a while, take refuge for a little from your tumultuous thoughts, cast off your cares and let your burdensome distractions wait. Take some leisure for God. Rest awhile in him. Enter into the chamber of your mind — put out everything except God and whatever helps you to seek him; close your door and seek him. Say now to God, with all your heart, 'I seek thy face, O God, thy face I seek.'

The more of us who follow this advice, the better for ourselves, our society and our world.

14 Anchor for the soul

The Bible is quite clear in its teaching about the mystery of God. Moses at the Burning Bush asks God for a name which will authenticate his mission when he returns to his people in Egypt. He is told in effect 'All that you can say about me is "I AM"', as if to say that the only proper way to address God is 'THOU'; the 100 hundred other names are all integrated in that personal pronoun.

John in the New Testament says much the same: 'No man has seen God at any time'. Paul adds his support: 'who only has immortality, dwelling in light unapproachable, whom no man has seen, nor can see'. The essence of the Godhead is unknowable. We Christians sometimes speak as if we had God taped in our thinking, rather than standing in awe before the Mystery of the divine Being. Eastern religions reprove us and speak of the untimate reality as the Void or the Abyss, unfathomable, inexpressible, inexhaustible, beyond our intellectual grasp.

We English Christians are not much given to mystical depth, but we have one spiritual genius, an anonymous writer of the fourteenth century, Chaucer's century, who speaks of the cloud of unknowing and warns us that God 'cannot be gotten by thought, only by love'. He adds that this cloud can be pierced by quick darts of love. We do not need to grasp God or explain him, only love him.

The gospels speak of Jesus as coming from the inmost heart of God to make him known, in terms of human personality and life. Paul similarly speaks of Jesus as 'the image of the invisible God', while John in words of deep devotion and theology asserts that he who has seen Jesus has seen the Father. Bishop John Robinson speaks of Jesus as the human face of God.

In the mystery of life and personal being, in the terrifying dimensions of evil both personal and cosmic, in the awful casualties of nature and history, subject as we are to the constant changes of human thought, the saving thing is to hold fast to Christ and not worry about anything else. No wonder that our forebears in faith thought of him under the symbol of the anchor.

15 Inexorable

Some people think that love is a sentimental, good-natured feeling that will give in to persuasion or pressure and let people have what they want or demand. There is an inexorable note about true love which will not yield to pressure, persuasion or emotional blackmail. It will stand for what is just and right, in an understanding and gentle but firm way.

Love holds up each person to the highest each can become by his own effort, aided by God's grace. It will never be content with anything less. All that is not good and true, beautiful and loving is a falling short of the highest and must be given up. God, who is love, will never let us go, never let us down, but equally never let us off until we become what we are capable of. Not that he will punish us, but he will never be satisfied with the second-rate. Prayer will not change God's mind or God's will, for love which would yield to prayer is imperfect. God waits for us to be the best we can possibly be, and waits for us to draw on his ever-ready help to become that which we know to be both his highest and ours. 'You therefore must be perfect, as your heavenly Father is perfect'.

Paul tells us to speak the truth in love. We must not be afraid to differ or on occasion to criticize, but this must be done from the motive of love and in a gentle loving spirit. Some friends think that if we love them we must agree with all that they say and do. The highest love will love enough to disagree when necessary, because we want the loved one to be as right as possible.

Ultimately we shall be judged by the degree of love we have reached and put into practice, as the parable of Lazarus and Dives, and that of the Sheep and Goats both warn. Love is the only currency that never loses its value. 'Love covers a multitude of sins', says Peter, doubtless remembering a moving incident in the gospel where he had heard his master say 'her sins which are many are forgiven. for . . . she loved much.'

16 Sharing and blessing

Jews, Muslims and Christians call themselves children of Abraham: Jews by direct descent through Isaac, Muslims through Ishmael, while Christians believe themselves brought into the community of faith through Jesus. Abraham is Father of the faithful to all three, though we do not yet behave to one another as members of one family.

Abraham believed he heard God calling him to go out to a new country where he could be free to worship the one God and build up a God-ruled community. He was confident that obedience to God would result in blessing for himself and his descendants.

More even than this, Abraham was to be a blessing: 'In you shall all the families of the earth be blessed'. He was to bless as well as be blessed.

Abraham's faithfulness to God was tested when he had to decide whether to put God as the chief value in his life, or the son through whom he was to create the new community and bring a blessing to all mankind. He was always conscious of God, sensitive to God's guidance, so that at the crucial moment when he thought God was calling for the sacrifice of his well-beloved son, he was able to hear God's restraining voice. Later, his descendants enshrined this priority in the greatest commandment of the Divine Law to love God with all our being.

In Jerusalem, as I stood by the rock of Abraham's faith, now covered by the lovely Dome of the Rock, I used to dream of a united annual festival of St Abraham, in which all three faiths could share the inspiration each had received from Father Abraham and pledge their obedience to Abraham's God and our's.

Such a return to God could result in God guiding us into the way of peace, and showing us how to bless one another and the world. It could even result in showing our three communities the right pattern of sharing Jerusalem, and making it true to its lovely name 'the city of peace'.

17 In the dock

The earliest form of the Ten Commandments was almost certainly short and direct, pointed out by the finger of God, and engraved by the hand of Moses so that the foundation of godly living should not be forgotten. The two tables were kept in the ark and carried round as a constant reminder to the people who had dedicated themselves to be a God-ruled people. Finally they were enshrined in the holiest place in the Temple. Year by year there was a festival of thanksgiving for the Divine Law and a great day of penitence and atonement for the failure to live up to it.

It is perilously easy to pay lip service to biblical standards. Jeremiah and other prophets demanded that the Commandments should be written in the heart, accepted as God-given, and binding in daily life. Anyone who takes them down into the heart, into thinking, motive and character, as Jesus deepened them, will be conscious of how far short he falls from the holiness of God, and will stand with bowed head like the tax-gatherer in the Temple, unable to mutter more than 'God be merciful to be a sinner'.

It is as we realise the perfect holiness of God that we see how far short we fall of his standards of righteousness and love. St Paul with his knowledge of people in the Mediterranean world summed up his experience in the words 'All have sinned and fall short of the glory of God'. Equally emphatically he declared 'God is rich in mercy towards all'. There is no sin so black that it cannot be forgiven, but although forgiveness is freely, immediately and eternally available, it does not operate until we change our hearts about sin.

The message of John the Baptist was a convincing one, arousing conscience and warning of judgement. Jesus took on from John, and brought a gospel of forgiveness, new life, abounding grace. He bore on his heart the pain of sin, not only the sins of individuals but those of groups, nations, civilizations and religions. As we look at our own hearts and the crimes and tragedies everywhere, we cannot but be dismayed. Only as we look at God, his will and law, his forgiveness and grace, can we begin to hope again.

18 What about *our* faith?

In the dialogue now taking place between people of differing faiths the members of each religious body are understandably anxious to be faithful to the original experience of their founder and to the inspiration which has guided them up to the present. Christians particularly are eager and insistent on their devotion to Jesus Christ.

The Creator of all mankind must surely be at work wherever his children are, trying to speak to their spirits in their own situation, history, culture and traditional religion. God, says St Paul, has never left himself without witness.

For Christians, Jesus is the expression in terms of human life, at a historical moment, of the power that set things moving, in nature and in the developing universe, and in the onward march of God's creating purpose. He shows us God; God loving, caring, forgiving, saving, perfecting.

He shows us in human terms the nature and work of the Holy Spirit in a way that was only dimly perceived before his coming. He also shows us man as God meant him to be, reaching a spiritual maturity which God has been producing all through the millions of years that thinking man has been on the earth.

To us Christians Jesus Christ is the Ever-living One, an ever-present reality with men, to lead, encourage, inspire and strengthen. He preached, embodied and established the Kingdom of God, in which men could know the Law of the Lord and receive grace to obey it in individual and social life. He taught that God's will was good, holy and loving, the loveliest and most effective thing that could happen in any circumstances, however desperate. 'Thy will be done!' is a glad cry of expectation, not one of sad resignation.

Jesus Christ tells us that the God whom he embodies is the supreme Reality, the originating mover of all that is, at work everywhere in the life of men, their cultures and religions, though our perception may be fallible, our interpretation limited, and our reproduction of the divine-human nature sadly imperfect. When we think of all this we see what a treasure we have in Jesus Christ, what a gospel, what a rich meaning of life!

19 The great priority

A priest recently said to his bishop that he could no longer preach about God, but only about Jesus. A decade ago the mass media took up the current theological fashion 'God is dead', yet very movingly the theologians concerned retained their devotion to Jesus. A great historian, who was also a deeply spiritual man, said 'Hold fast to Christ, and for the rest be totally uncommitted.'

The relation between Jesus and God will always be a matter of deep concern and vital importance: as we read the gospels we see that God was to him a great central fact, his absolute priority.

Speaking in his own time Jesus appealed 'You believe in God, believe also in me.' Today the appeal is 'You believe in me, believe also in God.' Even in the fourth gospel, which has the deepest and highest crystallizations of faith in Christ, there is the repeated emphasis that Jesus was sent from God, his authority was from God, he spoke the message he received from God, he did the deeds of God. Talking of his coming departure he said 'If you loved me you would rejoice, because I go to the Father, for the Father is greater than I.'

Do we Christians sometimes put Jesus before God, do we let our faith in Christ be a stopping point, or do we go on with him to God? Must we not go beyond the historical figure to the God from whom he came, to whom he went, with whom he is always present? The momentum of our love for Jesus must take us on to God his supreme reality, his sole authority, his great priority, the source of all love, grace and salvation.

St Paul speaks of Christ as the image of God: clearly God is the original, Jesus the human expression of God.

Our priority must be that of Jesus. Our faith: in the beginning God, God in many and various ways and in different times, Christ from God, God in Christ, with Christ to God, seeking God also in his world and among others, and finally God all in all, everything to everybody. Don't let our idea of God be too small.

20 Divine warfare

The Bible consists not only of God's word to men but of men's thoughts about God and their prayers to him. One of the Biblical terms for God is Lord God of Hosts, and God was thought of as fighting for Israel against their enemies. I was a schoolboy during the First World War and can well remember the prayers offered in church for victory over our enemies. At the same time our enemies were praying to the same God for victory over us. We both wanted to have God on our side, with very little thought of whether or not we were on the side of God.

I can well conceive of the armies of God as being myriads of spiritual beings and just people made perfect, all eager for righteousness and for God's plan for human society to be implemented, but fighting only with the armaments of God listed as truth, righteousness, peaceful intentions, faith and love, engaged in a warfare within the human spirit.

If we think of God as being a God of battles we shall inevitably be pugnacious ourselves, for we tend to become like that which we worship. But if we think of him as a God of love, grieving over the crying sins of the world, we too shall grieve over the sins of the spirit, those sins which afflict and ultimately kill our spiritual life, the seven deadly sins about which we do not hear very much in these days — pride, envy, anger, covetousness, gluttony, lust, sloth, all seven of them cancers within the soul, spiritual killers.

God's warfare is against these enemies of the spirit, which damage his children and cause so much suffering to others. And he must be against us as long as we indulge in them. Yet he longs for us to see the damage they do, and there is joy among the angels when anyone turns away from them and decides for the charisma of love, joy, peace, good temper, kindness, goodness, faithfulness, gentleness, self-control. Old fashioned piety? I would rather use the adjective 'eternal'.

21 Unfinished task

Nearly 2,000 years ago St Paul looking at the state of the world that he knew, came to the conclusion that creation was still in progress. 'The whole created universe' he said, 'groans in all its parts as if in the pangs of childbirth.'

This thought of creation still in the process of becoming is supported by the discoveries of astronomers that new galaxies are constantly coming into being, stretching out into infinite space. Creation is still continuing. I take comfort in this diagnosis as I brood over earthquakes and similar natural catastrophes, blasphemously described as acts of God. There are flaws which have to be set right, and the religious person believes that God is always working to do exactly this.

Cancer seems to be a flaw that has to be set right, as smallpox, malaria, plague and cholera have been. In my early years as a missionary I worked in malaria-infested villages and I shall always remember Sir Ronald Ross's poem of thanksgiving written on the evening of the day when he proved to his satisfaction the connection between malaria and the anopheline mosquito:

This day relenting God
Hath placed within my hand
A wondrous thing; and God
Be praised. At his command

Seeking his secret deeds
With tears and toiling breath,
I find thy cunning seeds,
O million-murdering death.

I would only change one word — instead of 'relenting', I would substitute 'redeeming', for I cannot believe that malaria or cancer are God's will. He is at work to correct and complete.

Paul urged that we humans should co-operate with God's completing activity: the created universe waits with eager expectation for God's children to be revealed. We have to assist in the unfinished task.

PART TWO

Towards Discipleship

22 Programme

I never cease to marvel at the spiritual perceptiveness of Jesus in his choice of significant and seminal passages from the Hebrew Bible. On his first visit to Nazareth, after the experience of his baptism and the 40 days reflection on his call, he chose a passage from the book of Isaiah which was to be the programme of his ministry:

> The Spirit of the Lord God is upon me,
> because the Lord has anointed me
> to bring good tidings to the poor,
> he has sent me to bind up the brokenhearted,
> to proclaim liberty to the captives
> and the opening of the prison
> to those who are bound,
> to proclaim the year of the Lord's favour.

It would be well worthwhile to study the four gospels to see how Jesus worked out the vocation that he had chosen, and which he so decisively accepted in his first sermon at Nazareth.

His programme was to be one of comfort, of liberation, the beginning of a new era of blessing. It is interesting to note the point at which he stopped his quotation from Isaiah; he did not include the words 'and the day of vengeance of our God'. His gospel was to be one of God's forgiveness.

The accent was on liberation, from poverty, from heart-breaking grief, from oppression, and I think we may say in the light of the gospels from the prisons we make for ourselves, in wrong attitudes, ways of life, and failures in faith.

People in the 'Third World' emphasise their need to be freed from oppressive government, from crippling poverty and disease; this surely is a right development of the scriptural vision.

The Christian Testament speaks of the freedom of the spirit, freedom from all chains that prevent us from attaining to the fullness of life, the maturity of personal being, and the following of God's will both for the individual person and for the ordering of society.

It was through the consciousness of God's presence with men that Isaiah and our Lord saw this vision, were ready to give themselves to work out its programme and even confident that it would be progressively fulfilled. We too, can accept it as the motive of life and citizenship.

23 Freedom-fighter

In his first sermon at Nazareth Jesus announced a programme of liberation. He believed that he had been anointed to heal the broken-hearted, to proclaim liberty to the inmates of every prison, to announce a new era of freedom.

Today the emphasis is on two external freedoms — liberation from political domination and oppression, and liberation from hunger, poverty and disease. These two liberations will only come when humanity becomes united and willing to live and legislate according to the divine will, of which Jesus taught.

Freedom in Christ is not freedom to do what I like but freedom to be what I am meant to be, freedom from any chains which prevent me from being my true self, freedom from the conditioning of the social environment in which I live, freedom from the domination of imposed limitations and external pressures, freedom, as an Anglican monk has said, from retaliation to those who behave badly to us. 'They react to life,' says Father H.A. Williams, 'as life has treated them. They are bloody because life is bloody . . . let us be free to be our own master and to live our own life, not to be merely the sport and toy of circumstances, with everything we do automatically dictated by what is done to us'.

We can only be truly free by surrender to the highest. To want to love God with all my being, is to be free from all lesser and deceptive loyalties. If I even want to love God with all my heart, I shall find myself wanting to love others as myself. This is what St John meant when he wrote in his memoirs of Jesus 'If the Son makes you free, you will be truly free'.

St Paul added 'Where the Spirit of the Lord is, there is freedom'. And three centuries later, St Augutine: 'Love and do what you like,' but what a stiff condition! So I have to be a freedom-fighter, for Christ-inspired freedom within myself, and for freedom from all the chains which prevent others from the abundant life of God's will, material, political and spiritual.

24 Divine handshake

One of the most moving insights about the meaning of Jesus was that of Paul: 'God was in Christ reconciling the world unto himself.' Christians see God in Jesus, something of the divine nature, character, will, activity. We judge all our thinking about God by that, though we recognise that our knowledge is not yet complete. There is more to come through commitment and prayer.

Paul implies that the world has got away from God. In Christ God comes in search of alienated man, constantly callng 'Child, where are you?' He takes the first step, holds out the hand of friendship, restores the broken relationship. He seeks until he finds, and then there is joy in heaven and peace in the heart of each one found.

The cross of Jesus shows that there is no limit to which God will not go. Nothing will put him off. In his earthly life Jesus welcomed everyone, equally accessible to the outcasts and failures as to the professedly religious and self-righteous. He stands and knocks at every door.

This reconciling activity was not to be confined to individuals, it was to extend to groups, nations, races. Paul adds another vivid metaphor to that of the rent curtain of the Temple — the wall of partition beyond which non-Jews must not pass was symbolically demolished by Jesus. In him human differences lose their divisive power — economic, educational, social, national, racial, denominational, religious.

Where there is hatred we are to pour in love, where there is bitterness we are to try to heal, where there is injustice to set things right, where there is class selfishness we are to promote and plead for the welfare of all, where there is racial prejudice we are to be colour-blind, where there is war we are to work for peace with justice.

Jesus saw the Father willing and doing all these things. He did them himself. He urges all to do them, and those who claim to be his followers he commands. And he promises increasing support, and quite a lot of travail, for the task of reconciling the world to itself and God is costly, and it has to be done afresh in every new generation.

25 Troubled question

One of the most poignant moments in the last hours of the human life of Jesus was that when he warned his disciples that one of them was about to betray him, one after another with troubled heart asked 'Is it I?' 'Is it I?' It was as if all except one was conscious that he might unknowingly betray the Master. All were out of their spiritual depth, realising that a moment of danger and crisis was near, only dimly understanding the thinking of Jesus, apprehensive for him as well as for themselves.

Jesus knew that Judas was not heart-whole, and was making a last appeal for his loyalty, without exposing him to the eleven others, warning him that a moment of bitter realisation would come when he would wish he had never been born.

I cannot think that it was the thirty pieces of silver that were the basic failure, that was surely a cunning way to trap him. Some Biblical scholars have thought that Judas in some perverse way was trying to force the hand of Jesus, to compel him to come out into the open, to use the spiritual authority that he so clearly had. Even then, it was a tragic misunderstanding of the mind of Jesus, whose sole purpose was to reveal and enact the love of God whatever might be the reactions of men.

If I am a disciple I must ask the same question as these first followers did — Is it I? Am I heart-whole in my loyalty? Do I put Christ and his Father first in my life? Or do I try to manipulate God to further my own career, blatantly, subtly or perhaps unknowingly? Do I put my own advantage, my own religious ideology, party loyalty, before the Kingdom of God?

Even to ask these honest and troubled questions suggests that I want to be heart-whole in loyalty. Suppose I fail? The first prayer from the cross covers both Judas and myself: 'Father forgive them, for they know not what they do'. Jesus died to prove the unlimited love of God, and also to prove the forgivingness of God — seventy times seven and more.

26 The completed task

The first three gospels tell us that just before he died Jesus gave a great shout. The fourth gospel tells us what it was — 'It is finished!' This loud cry from the cross has sometimes been interpreted as a cry of relief or despair. Of relief, certainly. But to say it was of despair is to contradict the spirit of the other words from the cross.

It was a cry of triumph, of victory, of faith. The task which God had given Jesus has been completed. God has been authentically revealed to men, not only in the life and teaching of Jesus, but in his death as well. Love has been shown to the uttermost, to the very end.

In Jesus, God has gone the whole way to show his loving will to men; in the death of Jesus he has made the supreme gesture of reconciliation. The forgiveness of God has been shown to be unfailing, even though men have brought his son and representative to a cruel and painful death.

God's character and love have been shown not only in hours when the sense of the divine presence, comfort and approval has been felt, but in those three hours of darkness and desolation when God seemed hidden. Jesus felt alone during that black period, deserted by men and seemingly deserted by God. Yet he cried out 'My God! My God!', still 'My God' — faith has been expressed without limit, and faith is most faith when it is threatened by outward circumstances and inner tensions.

The life and death of Jesus show us also a completed man — man as God in his creating love planned him to be. For the first time in human history, someone has been perfectly united to God in heart, mind and will, so the love and power of God can have uninterrupted inflow into him and through him to the whole human race with which he identified himself so completely.

'It is finished!' — the divine purpose has been fulfilled, the God-given task completed. The rest can be safely left in God's hands, he will have the last word. So 'Father, into thy hands I commend my spirit'.

27 Love limit

Jesus said that the greatest love was seen when a man laid down his life for his friends. He knew, for he was about to do just this.

There was another motive in his readiness to do so: his desire to show that the most characteristic thing about God is love and that God wants that love to reach every created being.

In the death of Jesus divine love and divine purpose became credible, for that death was not an arbitrary, pre-determined happening, but the ultimate, the unlimited, the most loving operation of love.

People sometimes wonder if the death of Jesus was willed by God. Jesus made it clear that he was free to lay down his life, he need not do so, indeed he was tempted not to do so. In Gethsemane his agony of soul was not just the shrinking from pain and death, though this was certainly there, for he was as fully human as any of us. The real struggle was the need to know if the cross was God's will. If he could believe it was, he could go forward not only in courage, but in trust that God knew what he was doing, that out of it would come spiritual victory.

Jesus knew that God's will was that he should exemplify God's love whatever the response of men. If they were to ignore him, reject him or even kill him, the Father's will was that he should not stop loving. Love was to be seen as unlimited and conditioned.

Jesus and the Father were one in heart and mind. There was no thought of a stern righteous God demanding a sacrifice, and a loving merciful Jesus offering it. There was only one heart, one purpose, one love. God so loved the world. Jesus loves it in the same way.

There was also one hope, that when men saw love unlimited they would respond. Love is like nuclear fission: it multiplies, it expands, nothing can stop it. In the end it will touch every soul, either here or after death, and every soul will find it the kiss of life.

28 The powerlessness of love

Many of us have got beyond the stage of thinking of God as a stern righteous judge, set on punishing people for their sins, and of Jesus as a gentle compassionate Saviour offering himself as a sacrifice to appease the divine anger. When we think of the dreadful thing that happened on Good Friday, we think not simply of the love of Jesus but of the love of God. Our minds are always wrestling to interpret Jesus, our hearts crystallize both thinking and faith in the words 'God was in Christ, showing the world the meaning of love'.

Jesus could have avoided being crucified: his life was his own to keep or to lay down. He was as fully man on the cross as in the rest of his life, and once nailed there he could not come down from it. Only men could take him down, as Nicodemus, Joseph of Arimathea, John and the Marys did when powerlessness had been accepted to the last gasp. Jesus chose to represent God, not by works of power, but by weakness and suffering, and by vulnerable and unfailing love.

We humans tend to think that the most characteristic thing about God is power. Jesus on the cross shows us that powerlessness is more so, insisting that love alone can change people's hearts.

We humans always want external miracles, and I am coming to believe that God is powerless to change the external conditions except through people involved in them. He works within the spirit of individual believers and in the unitive, co-operative relationships of people. Until that change takes place, humanity will suffer and God will be on his eternal cross. I must stand by the cross in the fortnight before Easter and let its shattering message find entry into my thinking, feeling and loving. God in his eternal love: God in Christ: God in men through Christ: love let loose into the world.

We have great power in our hands. We need love in our hearts if we are to help build the universe of love on which God has been at work through 1,000 million years and which took such a great leap forward one dark afternoon in Jerusalem, 2,000 years ago, when one God-man died to prove the power of love.

29 The finished task

Before Jesus and his disciples went out from the upper room to Gethsemane on the last night of his earthly life, he prayed a great prayer in which he clearly expected imminent death. In this prayer he said to the Father that he had accomplished the work which God had given him to do. Just before he died he uttered the great shout 'It is finished!', thus repeating the conviction shown in the prayer. It is good for us his followers today to think of the task laid upon him by God, shown throughout his life and completed in his death.

First of all, to reveal God, in death as well as in life. 'God was in Christ reconciling the world to himself', says Paul. Christ was to do that, whatever the reactions of men; stretching out the hand of friendship, opening the arms as widely as the cross.

It was also to show the unlimited nature of love. The response to rejection, hostility, desertion and execution was not to fail in love. To the very end, to the utmost limit, at the maximum cost, love was to remain undefeated.

It was also the proof of forgiveness. Those who had brought him there, those who had nailed him there, were forgiven, even excused — 'they know not what they do'. The 'penitent thief' was assured of a divine companion as he passed through death to the life beyond. We may equally believe that compassion and forgiveness were available for the impenitent one, as well.

And for Judas also, in his tragic misunderstanding, his failure in loyalty and his tragic remorse, just as later the risen Lord was to assure Peter of forgiveness for his self-will and denial. And for all who sin, however black and heinous the sin may seem in human judgement.

The cross was also a victory of faith: when Jesus for a black period could not feel the presence of God, when he could get no help from his emotion, no comfort from memories of past experience of God, he still called out 'My God! My God!', still '*My* God' in darkness and desolation.

It is finished! 'The strife is o'er, the battle done.' The final word is now with God.

30 Hymn of love

In Holy Week Isaac Watts' great passion hymn *When I Survey the Wondrous Cross* will be sung by 1,000 million Christians in almost every country and every language of the world. It culminates in a tremendous verse of devotion and dedication:

> Were the whole realm of nature mine,
> That were an offering far too small;
> Love so amazing, so divine,
> Demands my soul, my life, may all.

Organists, choirs and congregations conspire together to sing that verse more loudly and triumphantly than any other verse of that much-loved hymn. This makes me shudder spiritually.

Not for a moment that I would want to lessen the appeal and triumph of the event which the hymn commemorates. The crucifixion was a triumph of love, courage and faithfulness to the divine purpose. All this is evident in the words spoken from the cross: the first 'Father, forgive them, for they know not what they do', praying not only for the soldiers who had driven in the nails, but also for all who had had a hand in bringing him there, including ecclesiastics, Pilate, Judas with his tragic misinterpretation, Peter who repudiated him when challenged, and the remaining disciples who failed him.

There was the comforting word to the thief and the promise of companionship in death and beyond. There was the love for his mother and his provision for her care. There was the unfailing trust in God through a dark hour of spiritual loneliness when he still cried out 'My God! My God!', a triumph of faith. Finally his trusting prayer in the moment of death — 'Father, into thy hands I commend my spirit'. We are right to sing with heart and voice.

But the verse which I have quoted speaks of a total demand and a total dedication, which my self-knowledge and understanding of the words I am singing make me want to whisper them. For once I realise the wonder of what happened on Good Friday, I can never be the same again.

31 Great moment

At the moment when Jesus died, Matthew pictures the veil of the Temple separating the worshippers from the Holy of Holies rent from the top to the bottom, the earth shaken, rocks rent, tombs burst open, and saints crowding into the holy city in jubilation and witness.

The way to God is now wide open through the death of Jesus, the earth is no longer a cave of death, nature receives a deeper meaning, history is transformed, the living and the dead communicate, you and I are not what we were before. That is the meaning that Paul Tillich, a modern prophet, sees in Matthew's symbolism.

Paul adds a further symbolic event when he says that the middle wall of partition or hostility in the Temple, beyond which non-Jews might not pass was broken down. All may now come to the presence of the living God, differences of race, culture, religion, social position and economic status no longer dominate. We are all included in the love of the cross, all gloriously reborn and equal.

One sharing our nature and living our life has been of one heart and mind with the Father, completely obedient to the divine love, even to a cruel and shameful death. There was no barrier in him to God's saving love, which could therefore flow into humanity through him. No wonder Christ could shout from the cross 'It is finished!', a cry of relief certainly, but also a shout of triumph. The task of embodying the eternal love has been gloriously achieved, and a moment later in quiet trust he could murmur 'Father, into thy hands I commend my spirit'.

On Good Friday I should stand in awe and wonder, love and gratitude, penitence and hope, asking what difference I will allow that great moment to make in my life and what difference it could make to our troubled world if enough of us lived in its cosmic significance.

32 Breakthrough

The resurrection of Jesus is a cardinal point of Christian faith, and Christians often wonder how it actually took place. The fact of it is more crucial than the method of it.

If one sits down and reads the accounts of it in the four gospels, certain impressions arise. First of all there was a mystery about it. The disciples did not expect it, though later they saw intimations of it in the assurance of Jesus that God would take care of the issue if his death seemed both inevitable humanly and right divinely. Some of them were sceptical, wanting to be assured of such an unprecedented happening.

No opponents saw the risen Jesus, until Paul believed that he did so, several years later. The original 'appearances' suggest something unusual, a pause, as it were, before recognition. The factors of time and distance did not seem to operate in the usual way, but were transcended. Immediate presence, unhindered by locked doors.

Yet there were recognisable features. Mary Magdalene heard the familiar voicing of her name. The Emmaus couple recognised the familiar blessing before a meal. Thomas's doubt was set at rest by some perception of the crucifixion scars. Peter sees something familiar in the stranger who has prepared the morning meal at the lake.

Clearly it was something more than the resuscitation of a corpse. Something radical had happened, a transformation had taken place, the spiritual dimension was in operation, the death barrier broken. It was a continuing experience: more than 50 years later, John in exile on Patmos hears a well-loved voice saying 'I am the living one; I died, and behold I am alive for evermore, and I have the keys of Death and Hades.'

When did the moment of resurrection take place? Possibly the moment of death was the moment of resurrection, ascension and transformation to a universal presence. It took time for the facts to be perceived. When they were, there was another transformation — of the disciples themselves, of disciples of later generations, of a breakthrough into the eternal. The kingdom of heaven has been opened to all believers, with the hope that one day all mankind will stream into it. The doors are wide open.

33 Easter faith

As my mind wrestles with the mystery of faith, the reality of the resurrection and the meaning of the person of Jesus, there is a text attributed to him which supplies both a clue and a test: 'If any man's will is to do God's will, he shall know whether the teaching be from God' (John 7.17).

According to this, faith is not just the reasoning of the mind or a proposition in words; it is a commitment of the will as well. It develops from a desire for truth and a readiness for obedience, worked out in experience and experiment.

Put this in the Easter context. The tradition of faith, the hope and longing of my being is that Jesus is the ever-living one, the ever-present one, as available to me today as he was accessible to his first disciples, even more so because he now transcends the limitations of space, localization and time, as God does.

This means that I must think of him as present, always and everywhere. I must develop an intimacy with him that is spiritual, opening heart and mind to his coming, as he stands at the door of my being and knocks. I must be ready to spend time, quietly, reflectively, openly, listeningly. More than that, I must put into practice the intuitions that I believe come from him. I must let him lead me to truth, to the God from whom he came, and to whom I owe my being.

A twentieth-century writer urges us to do this, the great theologian, doctor and missionary Albert Schweitzer. In his book *The Quest of the Historical Jesus* (tr. Montgomery, pub. A & C Black, 1954) he came to the conclusion that we cannot get back to the historical figure in the sense of factual reporting and record.

He added:

He comes to us . . . as of old, by the lake-side, he came to those men who knew him not. He speaks to us the same word: 'Follow thou me!' and sets us to the tasks which he has to fulfil for our time. He commands. And to those who obey him . . . he will reveal himself in the toils, the conflicts, the sufferings which they shall pass through in his fellowship, and, as an ineffable mystery, they shall learn in their own experience who he is.

34 Fulfilled promises

The stone rolled away from the tomb says that death cannot keep him. The empty tomb tells us not to look for the living among the dead. The missing body asserts that the meaning is in the spiritual sphere.

Mary Magdalene is told not to cling to the past, however happy that may have been, but to go forward into the new era. The two friends on the Emmaus road find that when two or three are gathered in his name then he is in the midst of them. Equally he is there in the breaking of bread.

Locked doors cannot keep him out. He is there without Thomas, present to hear Thomas demand proof, present later when Thomas needs no proof.

He is there to forgive and restore Peter. He is with the thief who accepts responsibility for his broken life,and with the other as he hurls himself against the brick wall of fate.

He is on the lakeshore to prepare a meal for his friends after their fruitless fishing, as he provides spiritual food to keep his tired servants going.

He is with Stephen as the stones hurtle down, standing to welcome him. He is also with the young theologue who cannot accept the powerlessness of the cross. Later he is with Saul on the Damascus road as the lightning flashes.

He is not only with the two or three, but with the 120 believers and the 500 brethren,just as he is with the small group in the quiet village church or the large crowd in the cathedral, equally in some little wooden church in the bush or in some secret meeting place. Colour, race and class are irrelevant for he represents the creator of them all. He rends every curtain, breaks down every wall of partition, crosses every frontier, knocks at every door.

There is no place where he is not present, no solitary cell of hermit or prisoner. He is with the dyspeptic in the hotel suite and by the homeless alcoholic snatching an hour's sleep on Waterloo Station. He gathers up the fragments so that nothing is lost.

He is not only peace after storm, but peace in the storm. he always keeps his good wine until now. He is always fulfilling his promise 'Lo, I am with you to the end of time' and beyond He whispers, 'I am the ever-living one', here and now and always.

All that is Easter faith.

35 A time to wonder

Whatever may have been the Easter experience of the first disciples of Jesus, we who are his followers today have to experience him within our inner and spiritual being. Inner recognition rather than external proof gives us quiet assurance.

We tend to anchor him still in the physical, material, temporal, spatial dimensions in which we have to express our discipleship today. We go to the tomb expecting to find proof there.

At Eastertide I have found my attention constantly reverting to the experience of the women disciples who in sad devotion went to embalm the body they had taken down from the cross 36 hours earlier. As they stood by the tomb they found a question arising in their minds which they accepted as coming from the spiritual shpere: 'Why do you seek the Living One among the dead? He is not here, but is risen' (Luke 24.5–6). They went back to the house of the upper room to share this experience and conviction with the men disciples whose first reaction was to dismiss their words as idle talk. Yet they wondered.

Mark adds another insight from the women – the disciples were to remember that Jesus had said they were to return to Galilee where they would find him — Galilee of the nations, the way out to the world in a mission which he had laid upon them. They would find him in obedience, in world mission and service. Wherever they went as his disciples they would find him there before them, no longer held to Jerusalem or even Galilee, but as a universal presence, experienced in the spiritual dimension, in the depths of being, feeding them with spiritual food as truly as if he had come to cook a material Easter breakfast for us by the lakeside. Easter is a time to stand and wonder, and let him make his presence felt.

Several years after this first Easter morning Paul listed the first witnesses to what had happened. At the end of the list he adds, 'Last of all he appeared to me also' (1 Cor. 15.8). Ought not everyone who claims to be a disciple to be able to say this?

36 Easter presence

Many people nowadays only go to church for baptisms, weddings and funerals, or perhaps for the confirmation of a godchild, a responsibility accepted lightheartedly at the request of a friend. At a funeral we may still hear the words 'I am the resurrection and the life', declaimed dutifully and solemnly, which may mean little more than words read from a forsaken book, or occasionally said with such quiet conviction that they assert faith in life in the very presence of death.

To Christians Easter means more than the commemoration of a day when something unprecendented happened — a man, asserted dead by both executioners and friends, was experienced as present and living by his friends. Only friends who had known him could recognise him, as a child recognises happily the voice of a mother in the dark and trustingly snuggles down in a warm bed. Easter is the reminder of an ever-living one, present always and everywhere, which the inner eye of love can see and the listening heart can hear. Someone who at first seems strange, then faintly reminiscent, and finally recognisable by the familiar voice and by scars which no plastic surgery can disguise. 'It is the Lord', as the beloved and loving disciple whispered to Peter, in the Easter experience on the lake of Galilee.

'Why do you seek the living among the dead?' the women heard a voice saying to them in the Calvary garden, which went on to remind them of the promise of Jesus that after his death he would go before them to Galilee, Galilee of the nations, on the way out to a suffering world so desparately in need of love.

Spiritual conviction not physical proof is what the risen Lord demands, a conviction that arises from experiential adventure and awareness. 'It is getting long ago; where is the promise of his coming?' Robert Browning makes men asks in his poem '*A Death in the Desert*', the death being that of John the last of the first experiencers of the resurrection. The answer is 'He is here. He is come. He is with us for evermore.' In sensing his abiding presence, I can sing with heart as well as voice 'Hallel-lu-Jah', Praise be to God!

37 Easter question

The most telling evidence of what we speak of as the 'resurrection' is the experience of followers of Jesus in every generation since. People of all ages, different races, cultures and nationalities speak of Jesus as a present, creative influence in their lives, not just a wish that he were still with us in a physical body, but an experience of his spiritual presence, no longer limited by space, time and body.

In the power of that continuing experience people have been ready to go to the stake, endure years of imprisonment, suffer torture, without complaint or bitterness, keep loving and cheerful through years of physical pain, accept the growing diminishments of old age, face death without fear, indeed look forward to it with eager interest in what future God has planned.

Many can testify to recovery after failure, to forgiveness for sins against conscience and love, to courage in times of misfortune and difficulty, to growth in compassion and love, while millions are grateful for eyes being opened to see God at work or being ignored in the kaleidoscopic changes, dismaying happenings and hopeful responses. Many more find inspiration in daily work which helps to provide services for mankind and in thankfulness for the loving warmth of home and family friendship.

Through years of friendly contact with people of other faith, I have found admiration for Jesus, except when he has become a symbol for unloving Christians or intolerant church folk. Talking with them I have noticed how often they quote Jesus to support their own efforts in faith and living. They are not opposed to him, but they are vigorously critical of Christians who are unlike him. People are less likely to be won today by argument, they want to see lives changed, made lovable and loving, by a living relationship with one we claim to be ever-living, omnipresent, unchanging, continuing from the gospel days, and stretching into the eternal future.

This faces the individual disciple and any body of Christians with a sharp 'leading question': Do I, do we, in all the thinking, tensions, problems, tragedies, failures, decisions and plans, opportunities and adventures of life, behave as people who believe in the continuing presence of Jesus?

38 A great event

The account of the Ascension in Luke 24.50–53 is short and reticent; it does not attempt to say how the happening took place.

Jesus told his disciples that he came from God and was going to God. At his death he committed his spirit into the Father's hands. After his death, his closest disciples underwent a number of experiences, which convinced them that death was not the end. There came a time, however, when these experiences, which they believed to be of touch and sight, came to an end. From that time on Jesus was to be perceived through the spiritual dimension only. A quiet assurance of faith confirmed the promise that he would be with them to the end of time.

From that point on his first disciples believed that he was with God, in the sphere of eternity and power, in the place of final authority. The event of the Ascension spoke of God's crowning of what Jesus had done. The birth of Jesus is the symbol of God with men: the Ascension is the symbol and the assurance that Jesus is with God. And because the spirit of God fills the universe, Jesus is everywhere and always present with God, as he had promised to be.

St Luke makes three interesting points. It was in the moment of lifting his hands in blessing that Jesus parted from their physical sight. Always blessing — with continuing presence, never-ending love, unfailing grace.

Secondly, he says that the disciples went back to Jerusalem with great joy. Not anti-climax after the great 40 days, no sense of separation or loss. Just a great joy, and a great expectation.

In the power of that Ascension experience, they were regularly in the Temple praising God. There was no sense of hostility towards their Jewish fellows – that tragic separation came later. What had happened was all of one piece with the great things God had done in the past — Abraham, Moses, David, the prophets and saints, and now the ever-living, ever-blessing, exalted Jesus. No wonder they praised God!

39 Right-hand man

The occupying power which executed Jesus, and its collaborators, thought that his death had finally disposed of him. But his influence continued in a new dimension. He had already become a creative power in the lives of his followers, and this was to continue more powerfully than ever before. It was as if his loving dynamic spirit had been released by death to become a universal presence. His friends found his promise fulfilled: 'Lo, I am with you always, even to the end of time'. Wherever they went and whatever happened they found he was present, in this spiritual dimension which through him had become real to them.

The 'resurrection' was not that on a certain day in the early thirties of the first century a man had survived death, but that Jesus became the ever-living, ever-present, omnipresent one, not only in the external environment in which we live, but, if invited, within the human spirit, the culminating point in the whole creative purpose of God.

It took these earliest disciples some days to perceive this, it took a tremendous 40 days in which to work out its implications, it took a lifetime to experience its full effects. And from the moment of faith commitment, the task of changing human society into the kingdom of God was seen as both imperative and possible. Further, should their mission to the world result in death they saw the ever-living one standing symbolically as God's right-hand man to strengthen and welcome them into the divine presence. This was equally true if a follower remained on the human scene until old age with its decaying physical powers.

What follows? At any moment I can contact the ever-living one, converse with him, ask for guidance, receive enabling strength, be assured that God is always at work in personal lives and human history. Through struggles for faith, in the face of contemporary scepticisms, I can begin here and now to live in the divine milieu, being prepared for whatever God has ultimately planned for all his children.

40 The representative

Bible writers insist that no one has ever seen God; writers of the New Testament believe that in Jesus God showed himself in terms of a human life that everyone could understand. St Paul and the writer of the Epistle to the Hebrews speak of Jesus as the image of the invisible God, bearing the very stamp of his nature. Paul adds that we see the glory of God in the face of Jesus Christ.

To Jesus himself God was the central fact, the great priority of his thinking and life. He claimed that he passed on to men the things he heard the Father saying, and put into practice the things he saw the Father doing and willing. His aim was to be of one heart, mind and will with the Father, so that people looking at him might see God. We can say that he was the divine representative in human life, in immediate and constant touch with the Father from whom he came.

Another gospel description of Jesus was that he was Son of God, a relationship made clear in the experiences of his baptism and transfiguration, 'Thou art my beloved Son' heard at the first, and 'This is my beloved Son' heard at the second by the watching three disciples. The first and last words from the cross attested this conviction, 'Father, forgive them . . .', prayed at a moment of intense agony, 'Father, into thy hands . . .', at the moment of death.

Jesus is also spoken of as the first-born among many brethren, as if he were the older brother leading his younger brothers and sisters to 'my Father and your Father'.

In all these thoughts it is God who has the priority, in the relationship of father and son, image and original, representative and the one represented. For myself, whenever I think of God I think of Jesus, and whenever I think of Jesus I think of God. And if God is like Jesus, my heart cries out 'My God! how wonderful Thou art!'

41 Universal brother

People today are interested in the humanity of Jesus; they want to be sure that he was as human as we are. That is why, in an age when the focus is on sex, people want to know about his sex life. They want to be assured that he had to deal with the same temptations and pressures as we do, and that he was not a god in human disguise. The New Testament says that he was tempted in all ways as we are, yet without sin.

He developed as we do, growing in wisdom as in age to physical maturity. Luke gives us a lovely picture of him at twelve years of age, sitting with the rabbis in the Temple, so thrilled that he forgot about his anxious parents, and showing by the questions he asked about things he wanted to know what a bright, thoughtful boy he was.

He grew tired as we do, was thirsty, wept at the grave of his friend, sweated blood at the threat of death, felt deserted by God in a black hour on the Cross. That last incident assures me of his true humanity, and brings comfort when I am despondent and can't feel God near.

He often spoke of himself as 'son of man' and in many of the references it seems to emphasise his representative humanity more than the divine figure mentioned in the book of Daniel.

He speaks of God as 'my father and your father', thus making himself brother to us all. A New Testament writer speaks of him as the firstborn among many brethren, our elder brother who has gone to the end of the human road and can be a companion to us as we travel the same road.

People sometimes say to me that they can accept Jesus as the best man that ever lived, but not as divine. That is where Peter and the rest started. They were attracted by him, puzzled by him, but ready to follow him.

Try to imitate him and see where that leads. It will demand significant changes in each of us and land us in unexpected situations. Yet always in his company.

42 Lost, stolen or strayed!

I have always been interested in the instruction of Jesus to his disciples after the feeding of the 5,000 'Gather up the fragments that nothing be lost'. While particular to that incident, it seems to have been a general principle of both Jesus and the Father, that nobody and nothing should be finally lost. In his early ministry Jesus spoke of being sent to the lost sheep of Israel, and later added 'The Son of man came to seek and to save [all] the lost!'

As chaplain for a time to a children's hospital I was troubled about babies born with some congenital disease, and today reading about thousands of starving children dying before they have a chance to live I feel equally concerned. I learn from Jesus that these little scraps of humanity are gathered up safely by God, baptised or unbaptised.

St John in his gospel says that the purpose of our Lord's life and death was that he might gather into one the children of God that are scattered abroad. St Paul sees the eternal purpose that Christ should gather all things into one, all truths and all souls. In the divine treasury no truth, no act of heroism, no deed of kindness, no relationship of love shall ever be lost.

I would dare to believe that no soul need be finally lost, and that the door of each one's hell is never locked, and its other side is the gate of heaven. Many people have never had a chance to experience unfailing love or to come to know a God who understands the tragedies and mistakes of people 'who know not what they do', making excuses for them.

The three parables of the lost sheep, the lost coin and the lost son cover between them those lost through foolishness, those lost by accident and those lost by deliberate choice.

Jesus said that he had compassion on people, for they were like sheep without a shepherd to guide and guard them. No one will be able to seize them out of his hands, nothing in life or death can separate us from the love of God, which was personified in Jesus.

43 Must be contemporary

As one reads the gospels one quickly becomes aware that Jesus was approachable and welcoming to all who wanted to meet him. Religious people wanted him to dine with them, non-church-goers enjoyed his company. A leper felt the touch of his hand, a prostitute was not afraid to express her gratitude. A Roman officer wanted his help, a Samaritan woman wanted to discuss religion. People brought their sick for healing, mothers brought their little ones to be blessed, children came to listen to his stories.

He was approachable, never holding people at arm's length, easy to talk to, quick to find the right wavelength for each, the kind of person to whom you could confide your troubles, failures and problems. What he said to people had a salty touch, challenging them to go deeper, to change their attitudes and lifestyle. He was always trying to unveil the mystery and meaning of life and to assure people that the power at the heart of the universe was the power of a loving heart.

Those who heard him spotted an authentic touch with God; they began to feel that God was like Jesus and equally approachable and welcoming. He held out the vision of a better order of things, but emphasised that this would involve costly change of heart, new thinking, radically different behaviour, not so impossible if people could believe that God was always pouring in love into loveless situations.

No wonder then that people were pleased to meet him, get his mind on things. And every generation since has studied him, hoping that what he told them was true. Our generation, with its deepening psychological awareness, wants inner experience to confirm the insights of scripture, the traditional faith of the Church and the witness of Christians. People today want to see Christ embodied in human lives, they want to be assured that he is as contemporary today as he was in New Testament times. Sydney Carter has caught the modern mood:

So shut the Bible up and show me how
The Christ you talk about is living now.

44 Could it happen again?

Most of us would be a little frightened if it happened to us. There was enthusiasm, an abandon, amounting to ecstasy, which most reserved British people would want to keep out of.

There was a note of power about it, like being blown along by a powerful wind, and a fire of energy and love.

Most of those present understood what had happened. There was a unity of heart and mind amounting almost to a common language.

There was a sense of fulfilment of what prophets had longed for: the spirit of God was available for all, not only for gifted individuals.

There was a global promise about it. People from a dozen nations were there, and would soon be hurrying back to spread the new spirit in their own countries.

The regeneration of mankind had begun. Those present had become new people; all might become so.

Quick developments made clear the implications. A new ethic of limitless love was beginning to operate, which would ultimately burst the bonds of selfish groupings and nationalisms. The embryo new society in Jerusalem shared what they possessed: the criterion of distribution was people's need, not people's greed or even equal sharing.

The divine pattern of society had been inaugurated.

The great incentive, as well as the steadying safeguard, lay in accepting the control of the spirit. 'Repent and be baptized', said the main speaker; get free from the mistakes, the selfishnesses, the sins of the past. There must be a new start, new attitudes, new relationships, a new spirit and a new power.

Priority must be given to the Spirit of God, whose power and operation had been seen so effectively in the life of Jesus. He must be accepted as initiator, leader, inspirer, enabler. We dare not use him only to comfort us in our troubles, bless our petty plans, make a success of our own lives. He is to help us do God's will, not our own.

With him we can begin to build the world of God's will. And we need not wait a single moment. The Spirit of God is ready, if we are.

PART THREE

Towards Unity

45 Whose responsibility

A reader of these weekly meditations, commenting on my troubled musings on the causes of our present troubles, raises in a pointed way the responsibility of the Church, and does not disguise his own view that the Church has failed to save the world from many avoidable troubles. No one who has been a diocesan bishop would feel stung to spring to the defence of the accused, for his knowledge of himself, his own clergy and people, and our corporate falling short of the Founder's intentions lie heavily on his heart, more painful than the shortage of money, preoccupation with structures, bureaucratic efficiency and liturgical reform, necessary though these may be.

I am conscious of a struggle going on to extend acceptance of the command of the law of God to love others as we love ourselves to all the human groupings in which we are involved, and to extend to other groups the same rights that we claim for ourselves. I see also a struggle to make the Church a faithful embodiment of the spirit of its founder. St Paul likened the Church to the Body of Christ, the collective body, the agency through which Christ carries on his loving saving activity in every age. He also spoke of Christ as its head, co-ordinating and directing all its activities, pressing it to make its life the pattern for the life of the world.

If we Christians really believe in Christ as the Lord of the Church we should expect him to be at work on it. Malachi, the last prophet to have his book included in the Hebrew Bible, the Bible which Jesus knew so well, looked forward to a great day when the Lord whom people expected would suddenly come to his Temple. His coming would be a shattering, conscience-searing experience and he would begin on the clergy. Jesus may have had Malachi in mind when in passionate desire for true religion and worship he made his own protest and gesture which we call the cleansing of the Temple.

If this incident were studied honestly and relevantly in every place of worship tomorrow spiritual revival might be near at hand. Judgement always begins with the the house of God. My correspondent was right: the Church has a responsibility for the world.

46 Who supports whom?

Archbishop Laud, a great defender of the Church in the troubled times of Charles I, was very conscious of its failings. A prayer of his shows this critical awareness:

Fill it with all truth, [he prayed] in all truth with all peace. Where it is corrupt, purge it; where it is in error, direct it; where anything is amiss, reform it; where it is right, strengthen and confirm it; where it is in want, furnish it; where it is divided and rent asunder, make up the breaches of it.

In a sense the world is more important to God than the Church, for the Church was founded for the sake of the world. It was sent into the world to be an embodiment of the spirit of its founder. It was to be the Christ community from whose life people could deduce something about its Lord. It was to be a community of love, not only for its own members, but for non-members also. It was to be a servant community, serving and caring for people as Christ did. It was to be a supporting community, persuading people not that they must support her, but that she will support them in all the difficulties, opportunities and adventures of life.

People often say to me 'You churchpeople are always appealing for money, wanting to keep the institution going at all costs'. In their hearts they long for spiritual and moral support in the face of suffering, depression, death; they look for meaning in the changes and confusions of our time, in the temptations of materialism, unrestrained selfishness, failing standards. They want help in preserving family life, and compassion when marriages break down or when one partner dies.

If people find the Church eager to support them in all the pressures and demands of life, they will support it in turn and help to provide what is necessary to continue this supporting work. And if they do not we have the wisdom and love of God to enable us to carry on without it. Our greatest asset is loving, caring, supporting people.

47 A desperate need

For nearly 100 years Christian people have joined in a week of prayer for Christian unity. We have to thank God for considerable progress: the ecumenical movement, the Vatican Council, biblical studies; even the human predicament and a faltering faith, are drawing us closer together. The achievement of unity in India, Pakistan and Ceylon should be spur to slower Churches in the West, though let us not fail to salute Congregationalists and Presbyterians in England, nor under-estimate the near success of the Methodist–Anglican plan of union, nor thhe existence of scores of National Councils of churches and hundreds of local councils.

Yet many Christians desirous of unity are conscious of a loss of momentum. Perhaps it is only a pause for breath, perhaps a desire to face our differences at a deeper level. Perhaps prayer every week would remind us of our Lord's prayer for unity and the sinfulness and wastefulness of our division. It may be that prayer is not enough; there must be action as well.

True prayer demands that we do everything possible to answer our own prayers. An ecumenical conference 30 years ago urged the churches to do together everything that deep differences of conviction did not yet make possible. Great scope for advance here.

A saintly French priest, the Abbé Couturier, taught us to pray for the unity of God's will, and in the way that he will show us. Michael Ramsey gave us two valuable insights, when he urged us to pray primarily for the holiness of the Church, in all its members and in all its branches, and when he insisted that the unity of the church, when it came, would not be the victory of one Church over the others, but the triumph of the gospel over us all.

The world desperately needs unity and the Churches are hindering the coming of that unity by our continuing disunity, as well as delaying the progress of God's sovereignty over men's hearts and affairs, and allowing human passions and narrow nationalisms to exploit religious differences, whether in Belfast, Beirut, Jerusalem or London.

Let the Churches hear what the Spirit of God is saying to us, directly or through the angry, passionate, frustrated voices of mankind, plunged in an era of catastrophic change, and desperately wanting a different kind of world.

48 Signs of the times

Jesus once said that people were fairly intelligent in judging what the immediate weather was likely to be, but not as good in recognisisng the moral and spiritual signs of the times. Today our weather experts have become believably accurate, both about tomorrow's weather and the prospects ahead. We listen to their forecasts with interest and concern.

Are we as concerned in noting the spiritual climate with its warning, often gloomy and unpromising, but occasionally shot through with rays of hope? Do we see that although we can only take protective action about wind or weather, we can do something more positive about creating the spiritual climate?

Can we get any insight into what is going on in the human situation? One sign seems clear — we are being challenged to see that mankind must come into a unity, living together in what we now see to be one world, interlocking and interdependent. Even war has become global.

People from all races are much more in contact than ever before — travel, trade, migration, radio, television, press. We've got to live together, locally and globally. Segregation doesn't work, shouldn't work; we are all neighbours.

Individually we probably realise this, but the personal ethic needs to become social. The struggle for our age is to extend the second great command 'Thou shalt love thy neighbour' into the social, national, global dimension.

Unfortunately the collective pull can express itself negatively as well as positively, destructively as well as creatively, selfishly as well as generously. There can be collective greed and collective violence as well as collective responsibility and caring.

Jesus warned us that ultimately people will behave towards us in the same way that we behave towards them. If they have any moral principle they will want to delay any aggressive response as long as possible, but in the end they will feel impelled by need, frustration or self-protection to retaliate. That seems to be happening in a widespread way today. Our Lord warns us further that violence escalates, that our selfish aggression just stirs up the same spirit in other groups. We must disarm our aggressive instincts, morally and spiritually. We must accept his policy of reconciliation and work out corporate ways of implementing it.

49 The world waits

St Paul speaks of a new order coming to birth when he says in Romans 8.22, 'We know that the whole creation has been groaning in travail together until now'. He thought of creation as not yet finished. God's plan has still to be completed, man's dream has still to be fulfilled, flaws such as earthquakes and cancer have to be set right, men have to find the way to world community.

The pains are there alright. The question is 'Are the pains those of birth or death?'

The answer depends on ourselves. For men are no longer at the mercy of circumstances. We have the knowledge and the power to alter things. The writer of Genesis thought of God saying to men 'Be fruitful and multiply, and fill the earth and subdue it . . . and have dominion over every living thing'.

Certainly man has multiplied and filled the earth, so much so that over-population is a real danger. Yet, as both Isaiah and Micah pointed out, men can either make weapons or agricultural instruments: swords or ploughshares, spears or reaping hooks, tanks or tractors, bombers or mercy planes. The prophets looked forward to a time when the nations would no longer learn war any more. The choice is ours, to spend our resources on armaments constantly getting out of date, or on growing food for hungry millions with machines that are constantly becoming more effective.

The prophets demanded obedience to the Law of the Lord, with readiness to learn God's ways and walk in his paths. Men have to come forward, as St Paul urges, 'For the creation waits with eager longing for the revealing of the sons of God' (Romans 8.19).

Sonship, daughterhood, start with the individual; we have been given a pattern in the life of Jesus who we call Son of God. Then, the sons and daughters have to work together to make mankind a family and the world a home. Christians who claim that the church is a family, a community of love, the collective Body of Christ, should be living together in a way that could be the pattern for the world. The world is waiting.

50 Era of change

You may have heard the story of a veteran priest who had spent most of his ministry in one parish. A Friend remarked to him 'You must have seen many changes in your time', to which he replied 'Yes, I certainly have, and thank God, I was against every one of them!' Part of our present predicament may be due to our resistance to change and our failure to adapt to new conditions.

We have only to think of the radical changes and developments in this century, possibly more than in all the preceding centuries of human history — motor cars, aeroplanes, radio, television, technology, atomic energy, democratic process, national liberations, increasingly destructive weapons, expansion of trade, interdependence. The world has become one, but humanity has not yet found unity.

We speak of the two great wars of our century as World Wars, but have not fully appreciated the changes they have brought about. Field Marshal Smuts at the Peace Conference after the first World War said: 'the caravan of humanity is once more on the march . . . vast social and industrial changes are coming . . . upheavals comparable to war itself'. His prophetic words are being fulfilled today.

War with its awful destruction of life and property, its wastefulness of wealth, has caused increasing poverty of spirit and unceasing inflation of money values.

Technology is abolishing the backbreaking sweated labour of mankind and giving us more leisure, but we don't know how to use it.

Materialism is eroding spiritual values and the heart of man is restless and unhappy. Religion seems to have lost its vocation and tends to be conformed to popular standards and bandwaggons. Some of our theologians told us 'God is dead'. I would agree if they put the word God in inverted commas. Our ideas of God have to change to agree with his revelation in Jesus Christ and our intuitions of him through prayer and meditation. God is unchanging in his truth, goodness and love.

Our moral standards have fallen as they will if we have lost touch with a holy and righteous God, who said to the Jews and through them to mankind 'Be holy, for I am holy'.

We are in a mess, we need to be rescued!

51 The weapons of peace

The United Nations Educational, Scientific and Cultural Organization charter asserts that since wars begin in the minds of men it is there that the battle for peace must be fought. St Paul in prison at Rome had much the same thought when he said that the main fight is not against any physical enemy, but against unseen powers and ideas that are spiritual, against the factors operating in the minds of those involved.

He saw in the dress and armour of the soldiers who guarded him symbols of the only weapons that spiritual people may use: the belt of truth, the breastplate of righteousness, faith as a shield to ward off sudden darts of enmity, eagerness for peace firmly on your feet, trust in God's saving power as a helmet, the only weapon of attack being the sword of the Spirit which pierces to the heart of the matter with the insights which God gives. If the spiritual battle were fought first, with the weapons of peace, men might not come to blows, shooting, bombs, destruction and mass killing.

Zoroaster the great prophet of Persia who lived in the sixth century BC had much the same idea, for he pictured the life of the individual and human history as a constant battle between good and evil, between truth and the lie. The Buddha, living about the same time, said 'Hatred ceases not by hatred, but by love'.

The Bible insists that we have to resist evil, but with spiritual weapons. Jesus warned that those who resort to aggression merely escalate hostility. He urged that love has no limits and must extend to enemies, who are neighbours in the sense that they occupy so much of our thought. He taught us to pray for them, not against them, asking that both they and we should want God's right and loving will.

James, the brother of Jesus, added his description of the spirit of peacemakers: The wisdom that comes from God is pure in motive, peaceable, gentle, conciliatory, compassionate and kind, free from partisanship and insincerity. Peacemakers, he said, go on quietly sowing seeds which will produce a harvest of righteousness.

52 Rock bottom

Sometimes when things are bad and any improvement seems hopeless we hear the remark 'Things have got to get a good deal worse before they get any better.' Such a remark suggests that it is only when we experience the result of our present attitudes and actions will there be any hope for the future. We have to touch rock bottom.

Five hundred years before Christ Gautama the Buddha taught the people of his time in North India that there was an inevitable connection between cause and effect. He and other Indian thinkers called this the law of Karma. What I am now is the result of my past. There is a logical consequence of deeds. Good actions produce good results, bad actions produce bad consequences. The Buddha called men to create their own future by willing and doing right deeds now.

Over 500 years later, St Paul emphasised this harvest of deeds: 'Be not deceived, God is not mocked: for whatsoever a man sows,that shall he also reap' (Gal.6.7). One of the two thieves crucified with Jesus brings this out in his reproof to the other: 'We receive the due reward of our deeds, but this man has done nothing amiss'.

The diagnosis that present troubles are the result of past mistakes by itself does not supply the cure. But it has a positive hope, for it suggests that right and good deeds now will produce a better future, a harvest of good, as contrasted with the bitter harvest we are now reaping.

We have to apply this insight to our present situation. Does what we say or do now sow seeds of conciliation or seeds of further bitterness? It looks as if we in Britain have touched rock bottom. Are we going to stay there, or are we going to climb up again?

The Christian finds encouragement in two spiritual insights: there can be divine forgiveness for past sins and so a fresh start. There can also be divine grace to inspire and support our efforts to build a better and happier future. This applies equally to relations between estranged individuals and to corporate situations when we seem deadlocked in wrong attitudes and behaviour, and painful consequences.

53 Whose responsibility

I have often been asked by someone in desperate trouble or misfortune, sickness or grief 'Why has God done this to me?' My first attempt at meaning and comfort is 'My dear, I don't believe for a moment that God is responsible for this, but I am confident that he will be with you in it, not only to help you bear it without cracking, but to rescue the painful experience from waste, to turn it to good and bring out of it a blessing'.

It is blasphemous to think that all the tragic and wicked things that happen are brought about by God, that he determines everything that happens. There is much in the human situation that cannot possibly be the will of a good, loving wise God — war, oppression, violence, racial hatred, national and group selfishness, widespread hunger and disease. I am always grateful for Abraham, who in the sight of the volcanic destruction of Sodom and Gomorrah, with the death of good innocent people as well as wicked, stood up to the contemporary idea that God was responsible, pleading 'Shall not the Judge of all the earth do right?'

I am also grateful for the Buddha, who pointed out the causal connection between present and future, and urged people to make right decisions and do good things now and so produce a harvest of happiness and blessing. This insight was confirmed by St Paul — 'What a man sows, that shall he reap'.

Jesus was very much a Jew when he taught us to pray 'Thy Kingdom come, thy will be done *on earth* as in heaven'. Things are very much in our hands, and we cannot leave it all to God. For example, if we allow fear to dominate our thinking and escalate our expenditure on armaments, how can we go on praying that He will banish hunger and disease? We have in our hands both the power to create heaven on earth and also power to destroy human society. Let me express further gratitude, this time to Moses, who on behalf of God, pleaded 'See, I have set before you this day life and good, death and evil . . . therefore choose life!'

54 Any different today?

I have often stood at the spot on the Mount of Olives identified in tradition as the place where Jesus wept over Jerusalem. His love for the city and concern for its welfare are expressed in words that still move the heart: 'Oh Jerusalem, Jerusalem! How often would I have gathered your children together as a hen gathers her chicks under her wings!'

With the eye of a prophet he saw the inevitable result of contemporary attitudes and policies, unless its people and leaders recognised both the dangers and opportunities and were wise enough to distinguish things that promote peace and those that make for war.

With his heart overflowing with emotion, he looked down on the honey-coloured walls of the city, so beautiful in the afternoon sun. Just inside the walls was the recently rebuilt Temple, preserving Abraham's Rock and the Holy of Holies into which the high priest entered annually to plead for the forgiveness of God. Jesus would have remembered his first visit when as a boy recently become a son of the Law he had dedicated himself to his Father's business.

More than anything he would have grieved over the ineffectiveness of religion, its failure to realise the priority of righteousness and mercy, and that true worship depended more on its spiritual nature than on locality and tradition.

It was possibly at that moment that he determined on one last gesture of appeal and provocation, when in his zeal for true religion he engaged in a symbolic act of cleansing.

When Jesus wept over Jerusalem there was only the Temple occupying the view that so moved him. The pilgrim today sees the western wall of the same Temple, hardly ever without praying Jews, and just beyond it the beautiful Dome of the Rock built by Muslims to preserve Abraham's Rock, and still further the domes of the Church of the Resurrection, most precious to Christians. Does the living Christ still weep over the religious life of mankind. still yearning for it to give peace to the world and to draw humanity under the warmth of the divine wings?

55 Shalom—Salaam—Shanti—Peace

Those who have Jewish neighbours or have visited Israel will recall the word with which they are always greeted — 'Shalom!' Equally those who have Muslim friends will remember a similar unfailing word of welcome 'Salaam!' Both words are usually translated 'Peace', but both mean more than the absence of war or enmity. Each means well-being, fullness of life, happiness and blessing.

Devout Hindu friends have a similar word or greeting. An Indian swami who teaches contemplative meditation, a stillness of mind in communion with the Divine Spirit, always murmurs 'Shanti, Shanti, Shanti!' as he takes my hands in his, and I get the feeling that he means a quiet peace of heart, which he hopes and prays will spread to all my activities and relationships.

The good Buddhist often sits in quiet meditation and sends out in turn little impulses of peace, love, joy and compassion, beginning with his own family and neighbours and moving out to the people of his own town and country, to countries beyond, to the whole world and even to worlds beyond this world. The rhythm of peace, love, joy and compassion suggests the same ideal of fullness of life, well-being and blessedness.

Jesus said 'I am come, that they may have life, and have it more abundantly', the good life of the Father's will — freedom from hunger, poverty and disease, freedom from fear, relief from injustice and oppression, the acknowledgement of human rights, a relationship of equal value and dignity, a recognition of all the colours in the human spectrum, an acceptance of universal brotherhood springing from the realisation that we are all children of the one Father.

Such conditions of life will go far to produce contentment in the heart of the individual, happy relations with neighbours in locality or sphere of work, united nations — within themselves and in inter-nation relationships.

The glorious fact of our age is that such a world is now possible. The world has become one — in our knowledge of it, in ease of movement in it, in the spread of news and views through radio, in the extended sight of television, in interdependence, in the resources of wealth, technology and human planning available. All we now need is the will. God wills it — so must we humans.

56 Leading question

As I reflect on human relationships a seldom-quoted text surfaces from my memory: 'Is your heart right, as my heart is with your heart? . . . If it is, give me your hand' (2 Kings 10.15).

That question is a good one to reflect on when I am involved in difference of opinion, hurt or angry feelings whether directed towards an individual person or a group of people. It is 'a leading question', one likely to lead to examination of conscience and possibly admission of guilt, and so be a first step towards conciliation and a joint search for a solution acceptable to both parties.

Jesus had a pithy parable about a man on the way to court litigation, warning his hearers that there was a point at which reconciliation was still possible, beyond which it was difficult to withdraw. Bitter things may have been said or retaliatory actions taken which might seem unforgiveable. Most of us can remember going over and over a supposed grievance, imagining the angry retort if he or she says this or the further inflammatory action if she or he does that.

St Paul, who could be quick-tempered on occasion, urges his converts 'Be angry but do not sin', thus admitting the human tendency to get angry, but clearly warning them not to let angry feelings spill over into provocative words and violent actions. He added a useful piece of practical advice, 'Don't go to sleep before you have calmed your angry feelings'.

We might even go so far as to pray about the person or group towards whom our anger is directed. Jesus urged us to do just this about people whom we regard as enemies. I treasure a composite prayer inspired by Brother Lawrance, who spent 30 years washing-up in a monastary kitchen in the seventeenth century: 'Lord make me/him/her/them according to thy heart'. Such a prayer would be equally appropriate for the priest, the man in the street, those engaged in industrial disputes, national conflicts, cold or hot war, ideological scapegoatisms. The scribe who wrote the second book of Kings obviously thought that changed attitudes could lead to joint actions to deal with dangerous emergencies.

57 The gatherer

After the gospel picnic East of Jordan when a hungry crowd was unexpectedly fed, Jesus instructed his twelve distributors to 'gather up the fragments that nothing be lost'. This was a characteristic of his own activity and of the God whom he represented.

The little scraps of humanity that die before they have had a chance to live, the outcasts and the myriad casualties of history are all the object of his love.

St John in his gospel says that Jesus would die not for his own nation alone, but that he might also gather together into one the children of God that are scattered abroad. Jesus himself spoke of other sheep in other folds that needed to be gathered under the one shepherd. He also thought of the cross as a magnet that would draw all men to him and his Father.

St Paul speaks of a secret purpose of God that was hidden until the coming of Jesus, namely to sum up all things in him, both earthly and heavenly, all truths and all people. He would gather the whole of humanity into the unity of God's love.

It is Christ who will heal the divisions of the Church which are hindering the unification of mankind. This century has seen a great ecumenical movement among Christians, which at the moment seems becalmed, with the denominations reluctant even to enter into covenant to find the effective way to right unity.

Christ's ecumenical spirit must reach out further than the Churches, it must animate the encounter between world religions, drawing them into dialogue, fellowship and the service of mankind. This wider ecumenical movement will not draw all people into a triumphant Christianity, but into a deeper knowledge of God who is at work wherever people are seeking to know him and his eternal purpose. The Christian mission must be the prophet and agent of this wider unity; it should be the servant Community to other communities of faith, eager to learn of their experience of God, as well as to share its own.

Christians also see in Christ the shepherd of souls, meeting them in death and gathering them into a beyond closer to the Creator and Saviour of all, enfolding us in the divine embrace, and infusing into us some of the eternal love.

Above everything else, he is the high priest for all humanity, carrying the world in his heart, standing before God on behalf of man, and before the world on behalf of God.

58 Creating a future

Arnold Toynbee in his study of history listed a succession of civilizations that had come to an end because the people involved in them had become soft and comfort loving, and were unwilling or unable to meet the challenges of their respective eras. They had no vision of the future to inspire and sustain them. As one of the Biblical writers says, 'Where there is no vision, the people perish'.

The prophets saw clearly the consequences of present actions and policies and warned people to change their ways while there was still time. They spoke the word of God to their own contemporaries; they had a vision of the divine purpose — an age of rightness and peace, leading to happiness and prosperity.

One of them looked forward to an outpouring of spiritual power, not only on priests and prophets, but on all, young and old, slaves and free, a spiritual democracy. In that great pentecost 'your old men shall dream dreams, and your young men shall see visions'. I have often wondered about the distinction between a dream and a vision, and the assignment of dreams to the old and visions to the young.

Dreams often express deep desires, things that one wants to happen. As people grow old they perhaps lose the opportunity of influencing events, but they dream of hopes being fulfilled, and pray that they shall be. In this way they continue to play an active part in the spiritual dimension, the real sphere of decision and creativity.

Younger people see visions, ideals, hopes and goals for which to work, with half a century before them. The dreams of their grandparents can encourage them to hold on to these visions.

It is good occasionally to ask what is the vision which inspires and sustains myself, the dream I want most for the world — a world at peace, abundant life for all, a true democracy in which the majority considers the rights and needs of the minority, an all-embracing humanity which over-rides differences of race, colour, class and religion in the conviction that we are all children of God, created, valued and loved by Him.

59 Hopeless situations?

We are becoming increasingly aware of how much we depend upon one another. For years I have valued a prayer by a great American scholar and theologian, Reinhold Niebuhr, perhaps more in theory and principle than in immediate relevance and practical urgency. It runs:

O God, who has bound us together in this bundle of life, give us grace to understand how our lives depend upon the courage, the industry, the honesty, and the integrity of our fellow-men; that we may be mindful of their needs, grateful for their faithfulness, and faithful in our responsibilities to them.

In praying this prayer in our chronic emergency, I find questions arising in my mind of how the prayer of a few individuals can have any effect on such a desperate and widespread situation. That thought reveals a lack of faith in God, the eternal Spirit who created us all, with a capacity to know him, who asks us to co-operate with him in building a world of human relationships in accordance with his wise, good and loving will.

Prayer in desperate situations keeps these situations tied to God. It prevents God being pushed out of them. Every praying person affords a link with him through which the energy of love may be piped to the points where it is most needed. It makes us aware that we are all bound together in our common life, aware both of others and of God. There is live contact at both ends.

To affect the situation an adequate number of praying people may be required. I sometimes think of our common consciousness as being like a great web, spreading out to cover the whole of humanity, with each of us a knot in the web, able to send out impulses to the nearby knots and ultimately into the whole net of human relationships.

If I really believe in God, I shall also believe that he will use the link that I make with him and the human situation, realising that it may take quite a time to influence a chronic situation. I learn also from experience that quiet persistent prayer can reveal the hidden possibilities in seemingly hopeless situations, and suggest new initiatives and engender undefeatable hope.

60 Building the future

'And did those feet in ancient times walk upon England's mountains green . . . and was Jerusalem builded here among those dark satanic mills?' The answer to Blake's question is 'No', a definite, emphatic 'No!' So he bids us sharpen our desires, never cease from mental fight, strive with unceasing energy to build it here, inspired by chariots of heavenly fire. We have to build a new order, where none shall prey on others, where love shall be the motivation, where all shall care for each and each for all, where honour shall be given to service rather than to wealth and position. In a word, we have to build the kingdom of God.

Jesus called people to prepare for the coming of this new order by *metanoia* a change of heart, which meant not only repentance of our self-centredness and sin, but a change of direction, outlook, attitude, putting ourselves under divine management. He added a second requisite — faith, assurance that God is at work in this task of building the new order and that he will supply both the inspiration and staying power.

It is often said that man has come of age, that he has taken over from God the responsibility for building the future. Certainly the resources are there, the necessary wealth is there, the complex organisation is available. Poverty can be banished, disease overcome, slums replaced, war outlawed, racial discrimination repudiated, barriers between nations and religions broken down, injustices recognised and set right, mankind becoming united to live in a world that has already become one. Jesus must still weep over our failure to build the Jerusalem of our dreams and of God's design.

I find myself going back to a prayer which John Baillie, a great Scottish disciple of Jesus gave us 40 years ago:

I would call down Thy blessing to-day upon all who are striving for a better world; for all who are working for juster laws; for all who are working for peace between the nations; for all who are engaged in healing divisions and relieving poverty; for all who preach the gospel and for all who bear witness to Christ in their daily lives. Bless them and strengthen them to build Thy Kingdom.

61 What is happening?

Looking at the world today, with its wars, its racial prejudice, its class divisions and rivalries, its haves and have-nots, the widespread recourse to violence, the common psychological aberrations and the failure to find an ethical imperative which will gain general acceptance, one is tempted to ask what in the world is happening.

Jesus, as recorded in the gospels, warned his followers that there would come such periods of disruption, when people would be scared out of their wits, their hearts heavy with fear, not only for their own personal lives but for the life of mankind. We seem to be living in such an age now.

The gospels give us two pregnant insights. In Luke 21.28, Jesus says, 'When these things begin to come to pass, then look up, and lift up your heads; for your redemption draweth nigh'. Earlier generations thought that this meant the end of the world, but we may equally interpret our Lord's words as meaning that in all these upheavals the purpose of God is being advanced.

In Matthew 24.8, Jesus says 'All these things are the beginning of travail'. The word 'travail' can mean just 'suffering', but it can also mean 'birthpangs', and the New English Bible takes it in this sense when it translates this verse, 'With all these things the birthpangs of a new age begin'.

One age is coming to an end, perhaps because it has done its task, more probably because it has failed to do it. One age has failed because of its inherent weakness, its blindness to see the things that belong to peace, human welfare and world unity. Another age is coming to birth, but we cannot yet see its characteristics. In between the death of the old and the birth of the new there is bound to be uncertainty, misgiving, confusion.

Historians tell us of a succession of civilization which have come to an end, because they failed to meet the challenges of their time and lost their creative power. Christians are urged by their Master not to lose heart but to look with eager eyes for a new age, to remain steady in faith, and to be ready to co-operate with the on-going purpose of God as it becomes clear.

62 Is prayer enough?

Since the early years of this century there has been a week of Prayer for Christian Unity observed from 18 to 25 January each year, when Christians of all denominations in many countries have prayed that Christ will show us the way to the unity of his will.

The question may be asked why this prayer has not been answered. The answer may well be that the failure lies with ourselves rather than with God. Archbishop Fisher used to say that the churches will have to die to self-centredness if the great Church of God's will is to come. Is there any one Church ready for this?

Archbishop Ramsey has said, 'When unity comes it will not be the triumph of one Church over other Churches but the triumph of the gospel over us all', urging us to pray primarily for the holiness of the Church. If the Churches were holy, unity would soon come.

An American Bishop, Charles Brent, gave us this prayer:

Help us to place thy truth above our conception of it and joyfully to recognise the presence of thy Holy Spirit wherever he may choose to dwell among men. Teach us wherein we are sectarian in our intentions, and give us grace humbly to confess our fault to those whom in past days our Communion has driven from its fellowship by ecclesiastical tyranny, spiritual barrenness or moral inefficiency.

The prayer for unity *is* being answered. Some years ago I was asked to preach at a church where a friend was vicar. He asked if I would be willing to concelebrate with himself and the local Methodist minister. I expressed my eager willingness, but asked, 'What about your own Bishop?'. His reply was, 'Oh, he did it last Sunday!'. The divine urge towards unity is now operating at the local level, and conviction there will quicken the organisational discussion. All in all, this next week, I shall pray a very simple prayer:

O Lord of the Church, make us the Church of the Lord.

63 Follow up!

I find myself thanking God from a full heart for the resolution of the 1978 Lambeth Conference of Anglican bishops about war and violence. It is a comprehensive statement calling for careful study on the part of individual Christians, parochial church councils, deanery–diocesan–general synods and for informed, disciplined prayer in every Christian congregation.

It repeats resolutions of earlier Lambeth Conferences that 'war as a method of settling international disputes is incompatible with the teaching and example of our Lord Jesus Christ', and 'expresses its deep grief at the great suffering being endured in many parts of the world because of violence and oppression'.

It recognises the many faces of violence and the complex problems that have to be faced; it deplores 'the world-wide misdirection of scarce resources to armaments rather than human need', and recognises that the victims of oppression now despair of achieving social justice by any other means than violence.

In the face of the mounting incidence of violence and its acceptance as a normal element in human affairs, it condems 'the subjection, intimidation and manipulation of people by the use of violence and the threat of it'.

It protests at the escalation of the sale of armaments of war by the producing nations to the developing and dependent nations, a protest that should involve English bishops in some sharp debate in the House of Lords.

To me the most moving part of the statement is the declaration that Jesus, the Lord of the Church, through his death and resurrection has already won the victory over all evil, and that therefore Christians are called to the way of the cross as the way to reconciliation in all relationships and conflicts.

Protests, condemnations, appeals and statements are not enough. Unless they issue in long-term action and sustained prayer, they may do little more than ease our travail of heart and mind by making us feel that we have achieved something.

Usually bishops come at the end of ecclesiastical processions; at Lambeth they placed themselves at the head of the Anglican procession and in front of them they saw their cross-bearing Lord. Clergy, and people, including retired bishops must now follow — where he in his wisdom and love will lead.

PART FOUR

Towards Maturity

64 Two kinds of storm

People sometimes ask me if the incident of Christ walking on the water actually took place or if it is true in the spiritual dimension of life. I cannot be certain about the first part of the question, but I am quietly assured of the second. Again and again I look at the scripture passage (Matt. 14.22–33) at the faith enshrined in it and the gospel that emerges from it.

Matthew depicts the disciples making a night journey across the lake of Galilee. Jesus has remained behind to send the crowd to their homes and to have a quiet hour with God. A sudden storm arises and the disciples are hard put to it to keep the boat afloat and moving. Jesus appears, but they fear it is a ghost, and are only half convinced by his greeting: 'It is I, have no fear.'

Peter asks for proof in a similar power to walk the waves. Jesus bids him 'Come!' and Peter has the initial faith to get out of the boat and set out towards Jesus. Then he takes his eyes off his Master and looks at the stormy wind and huge waves, and his heart sinks and he is in danger of drowning. Yet he has the sense to call out 'Lord, save me!', and Jesus takes him by the hand and together they get into the boat. The storm loses its power and fearful hearts are calmed.

It is our Lord's final reproach to Peter which speaks to me most deeply: 'O man of little faith, why did you doubt?' I realise that the poor quality of my discipleship is largely due to falterings of faith, whether in the storms that come or in the adventures that in Christ's company I find myself urged to undertake.

He always comes in the storms of life, he always speaks through the noise of the waves, and he stretches out his hand to hold me up. With him I can ride the storm. Let me hasten to add that it is easier to preach and write about this than to put it into practice. The message is the same to me as Peter: 'O man of little faith, why do you doubt?'

65 When trouble comes

Sooner or later suffering, misfortune, trouble come to every life. Some of it comes from ignorance, some from our own mistakes, some as a consequence of sin. But there is a residue which cannot easily be explained, and we are tempted to blame it on to God.

People in trouble sometimes ask 'What have I done that God should do this to me?' The answer is 'Probably nothing,' followed by the assurance of faith that God is not responsible for the unfortunate happening at all.

St Paul, who underwent considerable hardship, suffering and hostility in his adventurous life gives us the key, perhaps not to explain the problem, but to enable us to live with it. 'We know', he says, 'that in everything God works for good with those who love him, who are called according to his purpose'. (Rom. 8.28).

Paul's faith is that God is at work in everything that happens, to bring good out of it, to bring a blessing out of it greater than if the original unfortunate happening had never taken place. When trouble comes, God's grace is close behind. God does not will or cause suffering but is in it to redeem it, as he did in the resurrection of Jesus.

Paul attaches two conditions for this transformation to happen: we must love God and want his will. Trust comes from love and enables us to draw all the strength we need for every occasion. Secondly, we must co-operate so that God's wise and loving will may be done.

When trouble comes we can react to it in different ways. We can let it knock us out, so that we lose all hope. We can rebel and become bitter. We can fill our lives with feverish activity, so that we have no time to think about it. Or we can accept it, trusting that God will make clear tomorrow what is so hard to understand today, looking with interest to see how he will bring the promised blessing.

In the same epistle, Paul asserts his own believe that in all the things that may happen we can be more than conquerors, and that nothing can separate us from the love of God shown in Christ Jesus. He spoke from experience.

66 Finding the way

Most of us, at different times in our lives, have to make choices or decisions which will affect the course of our future and our relations with other people. How do we decide what is God's will at such critical junctures, how find the guidance which Jesus promised the Spirit would give?

There can be no hesitation in the choice between what is good and what is evil, what is true and what is false, what is loving and what is selfish. Sometimes, however, the choice is between two seemingly good ways, or between two paths neither of which is completely good. Are there any guidelines which will help us?

First of all there must be eagerness to accept and do God's will without any condition or reservation when we discover it. Paul, physically bruised and spiritually broken on the Damascus road, showed this readiness when he cried out 'What shall I do, Lord?'

Habitual reference to God of all the problems, attitudes, opportunities and decisions of our lives, will save a lot of inner argument and indecision on particular occasions.

We should be ready to receive advice and insights from others but not allow them to decide for us.

When intuitions come, we should look carefully to discover any ulterior motive or reluctance, and be on our guard.

Patient waiting upon God should continue until a persistent feeling of oughtness comes. The prophet Isaiah probably had this in mind when he promised his hearers 'You shall hear a word behind you, saying, "This is the way, walk in it", when you turn to the right hand or when you turn to the left'.

Finally there comes the quiet putting into practice of the guidance received without dithering or looking back.

But supposing, after taking all this care, one should be mistaken? I think we can trust God to over-rule any child of his who so obviously wants the divine will and has the courage to start moving. It is easy to steer a car when it is in motion, but you can't do much with it until you press the starter, get into gear, release the brake and clutch, and go forward. Then you can go places.

67 Spiritual efficiency

Notice of dismissal has been given and he is ordered to produce his final accounts. Somehow he must provide for the future. Not strong enough for unskilled labour and ashamed to beg, he asks each tenant and creditor to sign a promissory note for attractively less than the amount due. In this way the agent is able to show a considerable total on the credit side, and also secure good will for his own future.

Two points cause us difficulty. We think that this shrewd action was the basic dishonesty, but it was the previous systematic mismanagement. It may even have been that in the understanding of the time the steward's action was permissible in a way that modern accountancy methods would not allow.

A second difficulty lies in the wording of the Authorised Version — 'and the lord commended the unjust steward'. Modern translations make it clear that it was his employer, not Jesus, who complimented him on his astute action.

The main point lies in the comment of Jesus that worldly people are more astute in their worldly business than religious people are in their spiritual affairs — more resourceful, thorough-going, far-sighted, efficient.

People know that for any career they need training, discipline, application, regular review and audit, refreshment courses, study of changing conditions. In the spiritual life we need training in prayer, Bible study, and worship; we need help in applying religious principles in daily life and work, and in seeing the relevance of religion to changing conditions, social justice and world peace. Above all, we need to understand and use the means of divine wisdom and grace.

At the end of the parable, our Lord adds a further pointed thought — we are to use our money in such a way that when money is a thing of the past, it will have produced a harvest of goodwill, spiritual character and divine approval. This thought could be salutary and seminal in our contemporary pre-occupation with money.

68 Late night special

Most people are not often tempted to indulge in physical violence. But attacked verbally some of us tend to be quick off the trigger and hit back defensively or even aggressively. So the words of St James, the first Bishop of Jerusalem, which many churchmen will be hearing tomorrow, strike home very pointedly: 'Let every man be quick to hear, slow to speak, slow to anger'.

'Quick to hear — ready to listen, to weigh what is spoken, to try and understand the emotion behind the accusing or hurtful words.

'Slow to speak' — until I have my own emotions under control and can give the gentle answer that dissolves the other's anger.

'Slow to anger' — because, as St James says, man's anger does not advance God's purpose.

There is a moving incident in the Old Testament where the wife of a Palestinian farmer, distraught with grief in the death of her son, refuses to be put off with the servant of the prophet. When Gehazi complains, Elisha, with perceptive understanding, replies 'Let her alone, for she is in bitter distress; and the Lord has hidden it from me and has not told me' (2 Kings 4.27).

How often I have not waited to understand why someone is pouring out a full heart in anger or grief, nor made any patient effort to find out what is biting the angry speaker.

St Paul reinforces St James, when he urges his readers 'Be angry but do not sin'. He realises that there are times when it is difficult not to be angry but he urges us not to let the anger spill over into sin. He adds a practical piece of advice: 'Do not let the sun go down on your anger' (Eph. 4.26).

Before you go to sleep, deal with the angry emotion, let down the tension, understand the one who provoked the angry feeling. In so doing, says St Paul, you won't give the devil (or the dark shadow in our nature) any opening. You may be angry but it will not lead to sin. And incidentally, you will get a better night's sleep.

69 Inner hunger

Halfway through Lent there is a Sunday popularly known as Refreshment Sunday. Perhaps it was so called because some of the less stalwart relaxed their Lenten austerities for the day. A more likely reason is that the gospel for the day is the incident of the feeding of the 5,000.

St John in his gospel speaks of miracles as signs, acted parables telling us something about the ways of God. He records Jesus as himself explaining the meaning of the feeding of the 5,000, and adds that many listeners found his teaching difficult. 'Manna from heaven' was an idea they could accept. but its provision through Jesus was not so easily acceptable.

The incident is a parable of God's nourishing of the soul. Through Jesus men can find the satisfaction of the inner hunger they experience. He gives the real food that people need for their inner life. It cannot be earned as men earn their daily food; it is a gift — from God in Christ.

In this acted parable our Lord says to us in effect, 'He who comes to me, follows me, learns from me, is guided by me; who lives in my mileu and lets me live in him, is united to me, lives by me, draws strength from me — this man lives on me, receives spiritual nourishment, which gives life, health and staying power for the soul'.

The gospel which Jesus spells out in this incident is that we can share his life, the life that enriches daily living and triumphs over death. When I participate in Christ I participate in the power of God who raised him from the dead.

The food which Christ supplies will keep me going through every difficulty, every temptation, every misfortune, every illness, every opportunity, every adventure, through life and through the birth of death as I pass from the material and temporal into the spiritual and eternal. It is offered and given freely and generously. Many thinking over the meaning of this passage of Scripture will be moved, either by their sense of need or by their deepening faith to say with his first followers, 'Lord, give us this bread always'.

70 Haunting question

An encounter recorded in three of the gospels is strikingly relevant to our meditations on the Ten Commandments. A young man of high ideals, living a thoroughly respectable life, comes running to Jesus, as if he had been wanting to meet him for a long time, kneels at his feet and bursts out with the question 'Master, what must I do to gain eternal life?', meaning the highest quality of life, full perfect life which nothing can perturb, a kind of life which many have seen radiating from Jesus.

Jesus quotes the Commandments summarising them in the text 'You shall love thy neighbour as yourself'. The young man replies that he has kept these for a long time but has not found what he has been seeking. He then asks 'What do I still lack?', a very rash question, for Jesus has a disconcerting way of putting his finger on a hidden or guarded spot. In the case of the young man it was his possessions which were his chief interest and value. Far better, implies Jesus, to give them all away, emphasising God's demand for absolute priority.

I must have the courage to ask the same question. What is preventing me from gaining the quality of life which God has, which Jesus obviously had? The answer will differ in each case. For many love of money will be the obstacle, or desire for success or reputation or power or sex or even a much-loved person. Though it is nearly 70 years since as a choir-boy I joined in the singing of my first anthem, I have not been able to forget a verse of Cowper's poem which runs

The dearest idol I have known,
Whate'er that idol be,
Help me to tear it from thy throne
And worship only thee.

The musical setting emphasised the message, for the word 'tear' was set on a very high note, and the third line was repeated, ensuring that both singers and listeners would not miss the point. The secret of full imperturable, imperishable, satisfying life is to put God and his will as the first place in my thought and life. The rest will follow.

71 Timely warning

In interpreting the Ten Commandments Jesus emphasised that it is in the heart of man that evil originates and that is where it has to be tackled. In three short verses (in Mark 7.21–23) he lists the hurtful destructive things that come from within a man. Among them he includes covetousness. On another occasion when a man asked him to intervene in a family quarrel about property he sharply warned him to beware of covetousness in himself.

In our age love of money seems to be the chief expression of covetousness, and the Bible describes this as the root of all evils, not money itself, but an uncontrolled greed for it. The Bible also speaks of covetousness as idolatry, making an idol of money, and putting the acquisition of it as the chief pursuit in our lives.

St Paul tells us that this craving for money not only leads people to do harm to others, but it is hurtful to themselves, and pierces their own hearts with fatal wounds. I am reminded of a wealthy man whom a friend and I had got to know rather intimately. One day I remarked to my friend that this man must be very pleased with the success he had made of his life. 'Yes', said my friend, 'but one day in a moment of sad realisation he confessed that in his concentration on money he had lost the love of his wife and family'

Having insisted that we have to choose between God and Mammon and having warned us of the damage that covetousness can do to ourselves as well as others, the Bible sets before us the positive opportunities that the possession of money can bring. The human heart is equally the seed plot of good, as can be seen in the generosity of people, some of whom though quite poor give a high proportion away and others make princely gifts for the relief of suffering and the advancement of human welfare.

We still need the tenth Commandment's 'Do not covet'. Having examined our personal attitudes towards money we can move outwards to make our nation a good-neighbour nation, both in its care for all its people and generous concern for less privileged nations.

72 Personality healer

The gospels present Jesus as a compassionate and eager healer who sent out his disciples to heal. There is an emphasis in his instructions, on casting out devils. Jesus lived in a pre-scientific age and accepted the contemporary idea of possession as a shrewd deduction of what was happening within the sick spirit. It was as if the spirit of the sufferer had been invaded, wholeness had gone, there was divided control, unbearable tension.

Today we think of inner conflict, in which one feeling seems to gain demonic power over the self. The struggle often becomes unbearable, and breakdown results. The sufferer needs inner healing and the restoration of wholeness.

Many of us think of spiritual healing as instant physical healing without the aid of medicine, instead of the healing of diseases of the personality — fear, anxiety, divided loyalty, guilt, escapism from responsibility or action, hatred, lack of confidence in our own identity and value.

These diseases of the spirit have their physical effect: worry leads to duodenal ulcers, guilt feelings to paralysis of will, overburden can lead to asthma, fear of riducule sometimes expresses itself in migraine and the desire to withdraw into a lonely dark, divided loyalty can lead to schizophrenia, uncertainty about our own identity and value may lead to violence or compulsive stealing.

Our first reaction is to deal with the physical symptom, rather than with the spiritual cause. I learn from Jesus that the cure for a guilt complex is gratefully to accept God's forgiveness; the cure for fear and anxiety is trust in God; the cure for the cancer of hatred is love; the healing of split personality is unification under the loving will of God; lack of personal value is set right by realising God's love and care for the individual; personal identity comes from recognizing that I am his creation, his child, infinitely and eternally dear.

Through the centuries the Church has thought of St Luke as the patron saint of healing, and on his festival day it prays 'that by the wholesome medicines of the doctrine delivered by him all the diseases of our souls may be healed.' Perhaps we ought to pray this prayer more often.

73 Cure for bitterness

Jesus was a shrewd observer of human nature. He noticed that when you give generously to other people they tend to give generously to you in return. 'The measure you give', he said, 'will be the measure you get back'. It is a very human reaction to do to others what they are doing to you. It acts both ways: if I am being grudging, threatening, violent to them, they will want to be the same to me. We can see how this operates in national and industrial relationships as well as in personal, and also how often the retaliation exceeds the original provocation.

St Peter drew the attention of the first Christians to the contrary example of their Master, who 'when he was reviled he did not revile in return; when he suffered he did not threaten'. He urges us to do to others what we would like them to do to us.

This does not mean that we have no right to point out what seems to us to be wrong or accept wrong treatment without protest. But we protest without ill-will, anger or violence, we resist in love, we put our case as persuasively as we can, and if there is some kindness we can do we do it.

Ultimately if we persevere others will do to us the good things we are doing to them. We must not let the unkind actions of others dictate to us what our reaction shall be.

Bitterness should call forth compassion. If there is an obvious cause for it we should attempt to set it right. If the bitterness seems quite unjustified our compassion should be even greater, for such bitterness is like a cancer in the soul, and hurts the embittered one more than the one on who it is poured out.

We may also remember the plea of a great Spanish mystic, John of the Cross: 'Where there is no love, pour love in, and you will draw love out.'

74 To be continued

The prophet Jeremiah, over 2,600 years ago, lamenting the seeming impossibility of people to accept spiritual and moral change, despairingly asked 'Can the Ethiopian change his skin or the leopard his spots?', adding 'Then also you can do good who are accustomed to do evil'. Later he became more hopeful, in the conviction that God would make a new covenant with his worshippers and put his law within them and write it upon their hearts. Old people like myself will remember the time when the Ten Commandments were recited in church every Sunday and priest and people would pray 'Lord have mercy upon us, and write these thy laws in our hearts we beseech thee.'

In conversation people often express to me their doubts about the possibility of inner change 'That is my character' they say, 'I cannot change it, can I?' Generally they admit the possibility and duty of controlling our selfish and aggressive impulses, if only because we have to live with other people and this involves adjustment and self-control, dealing, as it were with the symptoms rather than the root cause.

Talking to myself, I agree that my character has within it inherited tendencies, and I begin to believe that children inherit character tendencies from their parents as well as physical chromosomes. Character also depends on reaction to one's environment, the almost unconscious acceptance of the assumptions of society in which we live, as well as the influence of parents, teachers and friends. The important point is what use we make of these given factors.

I have free will and can choose and decide. More important still is my faith that every person is made in the image of God, i.e. that there is a spiritual ingredient in my make-up. This applies to all of us, and not just to religious people. We have an innate capacity for goodness and love. Being akin to God there is also the assurance of his influence within my being, which religious people speak of as grace.

All this is à propos of the growing violence that we see in life today, and the growing acceptance of it as inevitable. I shall meditate on this during the time ahead.

75 Generation gaps

The human race owes a debt of gratitude to the Jews for their emphasis on family life, begun with the fifth Commandment given them from God through Moses. It was somewhat unilateral in its earliest form, concentrating on the duty of children to honour parents, with no mention of parental responsibility to children. Later biblical writers, particularly Paul, developed this other side.

Religion to our Jewish friends is a matter for the home as much as for synagogue and church. I am always deeply moved when present at the Khiddush ceremony on the sabbath evening in a Jewish home. The supper table is laid ready, the mother lights the sabbath candles with a blessing of God the giver of light. The father then blesses God over a bottle of wine and all drink. He also blesses God over two plaited loaves which he breaks and distributes to all present. Finally the father blesses each child of the family, with the mother standing lovingly by. I often wish that we Christians had a similar weekly ceremony in the home. It might keep families more united.

Psychologists tell us that many of the psychological problems of later life stem from wrong treatment as small children. An unwanted child often suffers from this early deficiency of love, while an overbearing parent can sow seeds of other troubles.

Planned parenthood is more and more accepted these days. It has always seemed to be ethically and theologically right, for it implies a desire and decision to procreate at a chosen time, rather than let childbirth be the incidental or accidental result of sex intercourse. Disciplined birth control might also avoid many of the tragedies of abortion.

The developed fifth Commandment thus emphasises family love, equally vital in later life as in childhood and married life. I am now living, partly as resident, partly as chaplain, in a home for the old, the disabled and the chronically sick, where I find that the one thing most valued is the love of children and grandchildren, whose visits can never be too often.

We need to be loved. We need to love. We need God, for he is originally and eternally love.

76 Unexpected blueprint

If St Paul's great hymn of love in the thirteenth chapter of his first letter to the small Christian community at Corinth had been discovered as an anonymous leaflet, I would not have guessed that it had been written by him. For he was a powerful character, knowing his own mind, as hard as nails in bearing hardship and facing opposition. It was a miracle of grace that Jesus, whom he had never met in the flesh, should have made such an impression on him that he could draw up this convincing blueprint of love.

In the first three verses (1 Cor. 13.1–3) he declares that speaking with tongues, the gift of prophetic preaching, wide and deep knowledge and mountain-moving faith are of little value unless animated by love.

The next four verses (1 Cor. 13.4–7) gave a concise and concrete outline of practical love:

Love is very patient, very kind. Love knows no jealousy; love makes no parade, gives itself no airs, is never rude, never selfish, never irritated, never resentful; love is never glad when others go wrong, love is gladdend by goodness, always slow to expose, always eager to belive the best, always hopeful, always patient, love never disappears.

The translation from which I have chosen this quotation is by James Moffatt, a dour Scotsman and an austere scholar, perhaps as tough as Paul and certainly equally influenced by Jesus.

Somewhere among all the sermons I have listened to and the books I have read, I came across the suggestion that I should put my own name in place of the word 'love' in these four verses. The result was devastatingly humbling, and still is when I repeat the exercise. Try it for yourself!

The rest of Paul's chapter speaks of the lasting quality of love. One day we shall know as we are known, one day prophecy will no longer be needed for the perfect will have come, one day our partial knowledge will be completed, our childishness will give way to maturity. Only the spiritual qualities will endure — faith, hope and love — and of these three eternal verities, the greatest, says Paul, is love. So cultivate love!

77 Sick for the want of love

It is thrilling to note how the need of love is now being stressed from the human experiential side as well as from the standpoint of religious faith and values. We are learning that children need the warmth and security of love, and that if it is not available things go wrong in later life as well.

At the other end of life old people find loneliness a constant pain. As death comes closer we realise that love is the most valuable thing in life: the memory of past successes fades: possessions and money no longer satisfy. It is as if love was an essential ingredient in our spiritual and psychological make-up.

Sex is often mistaken for love, but many people are realising that sexual competence is not enough. There needs to be the mutual caring and self-giving: 'An I for an I' or 'My true love has my heart and I have his'.

Marriages go wrong; divorce may end an unbearable tension but there is always the scar. Divorced people may want to marry again for people cannot live without love. Many want to re-marry in church, not just for the respectability, but from a feeling that they need God's help to find what they missed before.

The opposite of love is hatred and this may be the explanation of so much violence, to hit out in compensation, in individual despair or in group resentment. The only cure is love.

Jesus said 'Love your enemies'; this can turn them into friends. The Buddha said 'Hatred ceases not by hatred, but by love'. A follower of Jesus, St John of the Cross, said, 'Where there is no love, pour love in and you will draw love out'. A follower of the Buddha, a Vietnamese monk, Thich Nhat Hanh, speaking out of the horrors of war in his country, appealed:

Promise me, promise me this day
while the sun is at its zenith
even as they strike you down
with a mountain of hate and violence,
remember, brother, man is not our enemy . . . .
Alone again, I'll go on
with bent head, but knowing
the immortality of love.

78 Brush up your love

Some thoughtful people who are agnostic about the existence of God put love as their highest value. St John in his first epistle says, 'God is love, and he that abides in love abides in God, and God in him'. So Christians and those who make love their ultimate have plenty of material for dialogue.

It is serious not to be loved, for we all need love, and without it are deprived and unfulfilled. Yet it can be said that it is even more serious not to be able to love.

How then can we learn to love? Once more John gives us a clue: 'We love because God first loved us'. We learn to love by being loved, by receiving love and then responding to it. In the same way we become aware of God's love and begin to respond. Our teacher John takes us further when he says that God's love was shown supremely in Jesus Christ. That was the chief impression which Jesus made on those who knew him.

John goes on 'We know that we have passed out of death into life, because we love the brethren'. Love being immortal gives us an imperishable quality of life. Still more 'There is no fear in love, but perfect love casts out fear': it does not arouse a feeling of fear in other people. Neither the one who fears, nor the one who arouses that fear has reached real love.

Love is more than an emotion, it has to be expressed in action. Here Paul is our teacher and according to James Moffat's translation:

'Love is very patient, very kind. Love knows no jealousy; love makes no parade, gives itself no airs, is never rude, never selfish, never irritated, never resentful; love is never glad when others go wrong, love is gladdened by goodness, always slow to expose, always eager to believe the best, always hopeful, always patient. Love never disappears.

If I put my own name in place of 'love', I see how dismally I fall short in the practice of love. Fortunately, it is never too late to take a refresher course.

79 Love is a seed

To Jews the most precious thing in life next to God himself is the law of God, sweeter than honey, more precious than wealth, not a narrow legalistic spirit so understandably condemned by Paul, and a danger in every religion, but a revelation of divine will, a wisdom in living which is always showing new relevance in new situations, a guide to conduct both for man as person and for men in society.

Jesus was speaking of the same thing in his teaching about the kingdom of God, which he described as a treasure worth giving everything to get, and as a seed with life at its heart and a tremendous power of growth.

My mother used to sing us children a song, the words and tune of which come back spontaneously:

If I should plant a tiny seed of love in the garden of your heart,
Would it grow to be a great big love one day, or would it die and fade away?
Would you care for it and tend it every day till the time when all must part?
If I should plant a tiny seed of love in the garden of your heart.

To accept the rule of the Kingdom is to be free from lesser loyalties, and to love God with all our being is to get our priority right. St Augustine used to say 'Love God and do what you like'. The condition he attaches to this liberty is overwhelming — only if you love God, only if you want to love as God loves, will you experience this freedom.

There is pain in love. There was a cross in the heart of God before there was ever a cross on Golgotha. It was there from the time when things began to go wrong and it will be there until the last lost child comes home. From Jesus I get the hope that the door of hell is always open and the door of heaven too. Each of us makes his or her own hell. God makes everyone's heaven, and Jesus promises a great celebration among those already there as each one of us, in weariness, penitence or in eager hope makes his way towards it, and finds the eternal Father watching to welcome us.

80 Sine qua non

As well as getting some idca of God from the negative approach of what he is not, we learn more of him from the positive way he has shown himself to prophets and saints, and most of all from Jesus Christ, whom Christians believe came from the heart of God to sepak to our hearts.

To St John, the disciple most conscious of Christ's love, the chief thing he learned from his Master was that God in his essential being is love, a love which reaches out to every human being, regardless of race, culture, religion, social or economic status, living in this world or in the mode of being in the sphere of the eternal and spiritual beyond death.

Everyone of us needs to be loved. If we did not receive love as children from our parents things go wrong in later life. Husband and wife need the deep personal love of one another, of which sexual love is a sacramental expression. In old age, when physical and mental powers diminish we need the love of children and grandchildren. When we come to our final birth of death, the only thing that we can take with us is love.

It is even more vital that we should love, and St John, that great exponent of love, says that when we love we become children of God, with a new kind of life that physical death cannot kill.

One of Tolstoy's short stories has the title 'Where love is, God is', so that where we see love we know that God is still at work, even if he is not perceived or given the credit for it.

A bishop friend of mine used to ask his confirmation candidates to remember three things about God: 'He will never let you go', because he loves you so much; 'He will never let you down', for the same reason; 'He will never let you off', not by way of punishment, but because he will never be content until you become what by his help he wants you to be. The original and eternal love will not be satisfied with anything less.

81 The importance of being loved

The most intimate of the followers of Jesus spoke of himself as the disciple who Jesus loved, and because of this experience he not only loved Jesus in return but came to understand the origin and the nature of love.

From his relationship with Jesus as a fellow human being, as an eye witness of the unfailing love shown on the cross and in the long continuing years of spiritual experience of him as the ever-living one, the conviction arose within him that the most characteristic quality of God is love.

John was conscious of being loved and so he learned to love: 'We love because he first loved us.' This is true of human relationships also. Most of us as babies were conscious of the love of our parents — the warm tender love of mother and the strong protecting love of father — so we began to love.

Without love in their earliest years children later suffer from a sense of insecurity and a feeling of no value. We often talk of children as being deprived: to be deprived of love is the worst fate of all. In adult years we come to see that the one thing we must have is love. Towards the end of life we see that the love of family and friends is of far greater value than accumulated money or achieved ambition. Love is eternal, it is the only thing that we can take with us into the beyond of death.

The logic of these reflections is to realise that each of us is loved by God, and to accept that love. Gradually we shall find ourselves beginning to love in return, God first, and then all his children, the whole of his creation. We shall see that the eternal purpose is to permeate human life with love, and if in the course of co-operating with this divine aim we find areas where there is no love and come across people who do not love, we shall know that the only cure is to pour love in, believing that then and only then will it be possible to draw love out.

82 Where it all begins

In the Sermon on the Mount Jesus shows how he expects his disciples to fulfil the law of the Lord and live as citizens of the kingdom of God. He takes four of the Ten Commandments — no murder, no stealing, no adultery, no false witness — and shows how these begin in thought and motive. For example, with the prohibition of murder he warns against letting anger get out of control, against imflammatory insults, against despising people and so regarding them as of no value and therefore dispensable. These three dispositions of mind, he infers, can lead to murder and must therefore be curbed at their starting point. The Divine Law has to be taken down into motivation and expressed in character. In that way only can it be effectively obeyed.

Jesus worked this out further with his disciples: out of the heart of man come evil thoughts, fornication, theft, murder, adultery, coveting, wickedness, deceit, licentiousness, envy, slander, pride, foolishness.

This penetrating analysis always moves me to close scrutiny of what is going on in the depths of the heart and reminds me of a prayer of the psalmist: 'Search me, O God, and know my heart! Try me and know my thoughts! And see if there be any wicked way in me.'

The heart of man in Biblical thinking is not just the emotional side of his nature. It is the very core of his being, what he really is. It is here that character is fashioned, and it is here in his spirit that the seed of divine likeness is planted. We are capable of developing into the image of God, and if the Christian wants to know what this means he has only to look at the life of Jesus, which shows us God and also men.

Paul makes clear the choices facing us. After drawing up a list of sins remarkably similar to that of Jesus, he makes the point that the heart can also be the seedbed of lovely god-like things: the harvest of the Spirit is love, joy, peace, patience, kindness, goodness, faithfulness, gentleness, self-control.

83 Impossible standard?

The Sermon on the Mount was addressed to disciples so it is understandable that the standards should be high. To some would-be followers they may seem impossibly so, notably that in Matt. 5.48: 'You therefore shall be perfect, as your heavenly Father is perfect.'

The text comes at the end of a parapraph dealing with our attitudes towards those whom we may regard as enemies or who might regard us as such. Love is to have no limit, it is to reach out to enemies as well as friends; duty, courtesy and kindness are not to be reserved for those who will reciprocate. This is the perfection of neighbourly love, for enemies are neighbours in that they occupy so much of our time and stir up a good deal of our emotion.

It may seem impossible but God is a God of grace, a giving God, who promises the strength to carry out his commands.

We put ourselves under the authority of Jesus Christ who brought divine truth and grace into human life, who embodied both. Under his training we can break our personal best so far. Even to want to do so is an acceptable starting point.

St Paul carries on the thought in that most personal letter to the Christians at Philippi; 'My friends, I have not yet reached perfection but I press on . . . forgetting what is behind me and reaching out for that which lies ahead. I press towards the goal to win the prize which is God's call to the life above, in Christ Jesus.' (Phil. 3.12–14).

'Forgetting what is behind' — the mistakes, failures and sins of the past, the falling short of the divine standards, even our limited achievements, not just forgetting them but accepting God's forgiveness for them, and our own.

'Reaching out to that which is ahead' — growing towards spiritual maturity, measured by nothing less than the full stature of Christ, all the time keeping an eye on Jesus 'on whom faith depends from start to finish.'

PART FIVE

Towards Eternity

84 A vital question

For some years past my chief interest has been the study and practice of prayer, and I always enjoy a session with a group of people who are willing to face the difficulties frankly, expose their own doubts and ask the questions to which they would like answers. A question that frequently arises is 'Is it any good praying if I am not sure that God exists?'

Hans Küng the great German theologian has recently had published a book of 750 pages dealing with this very question. It cost £12 (at the time of writing) but I consider it worth every penny to get some light on the most important question in life. He studies the conclusions and arguments of the well-known atheistic philosophers, and he comes to the conclusion that the existence of God cannot be proved by science or logical argument.

But neither can it be disproved; it can be verified. We have therefore to choose, to decide, to live our lives in the faith that God does exist, assuming that he comes, speaks, acts, forgives, saves, guides and strenghtens, is always and everywhere present. In short we have to wager our lives and see what happens.

There are two conditions to his experiment of verification. The first is that we must give it a fair chance. At every step, we must be ready to take the next step; there must be no reserved subjects, the whole of our thinking and behaviour must be committed. The second condition is that we must be ready to give the experiment a fair chance. A year might be a reasonable time to devote to the exercise.

We would be wise to study the experience of people in the Bible, stretching over 1000 years, acknowledging that there is much human thinking in that collection of writings, but every so often a nugget of pure spiritual gold. The judgement of others may confirm or disprove our original assumption. They may see a new influence, a real change in our lives, or they may not. My advice is to take the next book token to the nearest bookshop, buy Küng's book and make sure you get your money's worth out of it.

Hans Küng, *Does God Exist?* (Collins), 1980.

85 A good question

If God exists, and if we bank our lives on the faith that he does, then prayer, which can be defined as our relationship with him, must be our first priority, the most important activity in which we engage. People who are concerned about the state of the world and eager about the happiness of humanity, sometimes question this. 'Isn't prayer a waste of time?', they ask 'and wouldn't it be better to spend the time in working for human welfare, social justice and world peace?'

Jesus taught us to pray and work that the kingdom of God should come here and now, on earth as it is in heaven. The activity of prayer helps us to understand the kind of world that God wants, sets before us the goal towards which to work, makes clear the obstacles in its way, due mainly to personal or corporate selfishness, somehow strengthens us to go on working in the face of difficulty and failure, and helps us to commend the cause by the kind of people we can become.

A Biblical writer warns us that our actions prove our faith, and teachers with spiritual insight insist that we have to do everything in our power to answer our own prayers, if we expect God to act. So prayer is not opting out of the struggle or retiring into a quiet backwater where the pains of the world are no longer felt. On the contrary, prayer makes us feel the world's pain more keenly, but at the same time makes us conscious of the infinite compassion of God.

So I go to God, to be inspired, to be guided by his wisdom, to be charged and re-charged with his love, to be sustained when my fearful heart faints, to be helped to continue when hope is deferred and every effort seems doomed to failure. Then I can return to the heat of the battlefield, quietly confident that there is a power working for righteousness and love, who holds the whole world in his heart and hands.

86 An honest question

I am often asked and indeed I often ask myself the question 'Is it any good praying when I don't feel like it?' There are times when I am conscious of the presence of God, and other times when the heart is warm with the remembrance of God's goodness and sustaining help in the past, so that it is easy to pray. There are other times when the heart seems cold and dry, and prayer is difficult.

My question can best be answered by recalling an experience when I was a rural priest in a group of villages in the Irrawaddy Delta 50 years ago. A senior missionary and I had arrived at a riverside village just before sunset. We visited the homes of the Christians, tried to help any sick villagers, and later gathered in the bamboo school-cum-church. We squatted crosslegged on the floor round a smokey hurricane lamp. My companion gave a short talk dealing with this question. 'Imagine', he said, 'a son who has gone to live in a village upstream. Every Sunday he paddles his canoe to his parents' village. One week, however, he feels out of sorts and says to himself "I won't go today, they won't miss me". A little later he feels that his old mother might fear that he was ill so he gets into his canoe and is only an hour late.' 'Imagine', continued my senior friend, 'the parents talking together after the son has gone back. "You know our son was under the weather this week, it looks like malaria coming on. But how good of him to come all the same! How fortunate we are to have such a loving son!"' The speaker concluded by saying that God is like that. He is so pleased that we pray when prayer is difficult, and the heart doesn't seem to be in it.

At such times God knows that he may not have the full attention of the mind or the warmth of the heart, but he has our wills. And if he has our wills, he can do anything with us and through us.

87 A timely question

Many people today live busy lives and are conscious of the pressure of time, so that even if they recognise the need to pray, wonder if they can find adequate quiet time for prayer. I think of mothers of families, who have to get husbands off to work and children to school, clear up after breakfast and perhaps do a full or part-time job, return to cook the evening meal and retire tired out at a late hour to bed.

Such people may be helped by the example of Brother Lawrence, who after serving as a soldier and as a footman in a wealthy family became a lay brother in a monastery in Paris. There he was set to wash up the dishes and help with the cooking. He wrote a series of letters in which he explained his practice of the presence of God.

He thought of God as always with him and carried on a silent conversation with God and finally reached a condition in which his times of prayer were no different to other times. He was always conscious of God's presence with him. A regular short prayer of his was 'Lord, make me according to your heart'.

Life today may be more noisy and hurried than it was for Lawrence 300 years ago, but it may be possible to spend a couple of minutes from time to time when we relax and let the peace and strength of God flow into us, claiming the promise 'Come to me all who are weary and heavy laden and I will refresh you'. Or we may shoot up an arrow prayer to God, which may be little more than 'Father, dear Father!' Or when doing a routine duty talk to him as to a companion alongside.

In the spiritual dimension time does not dominate as it does in the physical. A touch with God can bring a peaceful heart, and give us the right tempo, show us the right spirit in which to relate to other people, and so save both time and friction.

88 A realistic question

Our lives today are so organised and social groupings so large and human questions so complex, that the individual may well wonder what one person can do or how effective his or her prayers may be in the big issues that face us today.

In the pattern prayer that Jesus gave his followers he taught us first of all to pray for three great things — the true knowledge of himself, the rule of his kingdom and the fulfilment of his will, universal blessings which could make a heaven of earth.

Natural disasters happen, cruel and tragic things are done, things seem to get out of hand, God's hand as well as ours. What can my prayer or action do? The first answer to this realistic question is that prayer helps to keep such situations tied to God and prevents him being pushed out.

A second thought is that most man-made situations arise from wrong attitudes within the minds and spirits of men, so that the struggle is basically a spiritual one. Our battle, as St Paul reminds us, is not just against human foes, but against wrong attitudes and selfish policies which lead to tragic and evil consequences. Yet if evil is infectious, good can also be so. I have to ask myself if I am on God's side, eager to create the kind of world that he wants.

Somehow we all share the same human nature; we are knit together in a web of relationships, and impulses of good can go out from the little knot in the fabric that is myself. I am encouraged further by the homely point made by Jesus, that it only takes a small amount of yeast to leaven a whole loaf. An Indian teacher of prayer once said to me that if 10 per cent of us were really dedicated in life and action in prayer, miracles would soon begin to happen in human society. So in spite of occasional doubts I shall continue to pray 'Thy kingdom come! Thy will be done! — on earth as in heaven.'

89 An angry question

I am sometimes asked by people who want to pray and live a God-like life if it is any good praying when I am angry with God or other people. This question started to bother me 70 years ago when as a young choirboy I joined in singing some of the bitter and revengeful verses of the poets who wrote the psalms. Today we usually leave out such psalms or verses.

Constant and perhaps more mature reflection now suggests a more positive thought — that if there is one person in the world with whom it is safe to pour out the bitterness of the heart it is God. In any case, before him all hearts are open and all feelings known.

I sometimes think that the outbursts of anger against God or men, is like the lancing of a boil which releases the unhealthy and painful pus, and so brings healing. Some of the prophets and psalmists, who did not hide their hurt and angry feelings ended up by praying for those about whom they felt so bitter. There is frequent reference in the Bible to God's anger; it is not self-regarding anger, but the unrelenting opposition of God towards the evil that is spoiling his children and his world.

We sometimes claim that our anger is righteous, but self-knowledge tells me that this is so seldom the case that it would be wiser not to claim it. St Paul urged his friends 'be angry and sin not', don't let your anger spill over into violent words or actions. He further urged that we should defuse our anger before going to sleep. I find that if I don't do so, my sleep is uneasy with recurring recriminations. In the pattern prayer of Jesus we are warned that we cannot expect God's forgiveness unless we too are ready to forgive.

In one way anger suggests that we care desperately about something. But it needs to be cleansed so that it loses its hurtful and destructive impulse, and then it can continue as a passion for the good, loving and wise will of God, for oneself, other people and an order of human society which comes closer to it.

90 Getting re-charged

It is good that religious people who make a practice of prayer should face up to the criticisms of others, and to their own occasional misgivings. It is equally important to pay attention to the experience of people, past and present, who have discovered the effects of prayer.

The poets who wrote the psalms experienced periods of dryness and moments of despair which they interpreted as a deep desire or thirst for God. They likened their condition to dry parched ground under a tropical sun, waiting for the refreshing, life-giving rain. When I feel like that, as I do from time to time, I remember the psalmist, who having experienced that spiritual thirst, prayed 'All my fresh springs shall be in Thee', and repeat it to myself and God a dozen times or more.

In these modern days people may find it more helpful to think of themselves as a run-down battery which needs re-charging regularly and sometimes urgently. Prayer is the link with God along which our need is expressed to him and his renewing power made available to us.

An American hymn writer has expressed this in a verse that I pray often:

Discouraged in the work of life,
Disheartened by its load,
Shamed by its failures or its fears,
I sink beside the road;
But let me only think of thee,
And then new hope springs up in me.

A Jewish prophet put it even more positively: 'They that wait upon the Lord shall renew their strength, they shall mount up with wings like eagles, they shall run and not be weary, they shall walk and not faint.' When quick decision and action are needed, when I have to keep going under pressure, when there are long stretches of unexciting routine, prayer will keep me going.

91 Hidden presence

I sometimes wonder how I would react if I had to undergo solitary confinement, either as punishment for some offence against society, or for the sake of conscience, when I felt I had to protest against what seemed to me the wrong attitudes or actions of people in power.

I tremble to think how I would endure being cut off from human companionship, newspapers, radio, books, letters, the warmth and encouragement of visits from friends, with perhaps psychological cruelty and physical torture. I have the feeling that I would quickly cry out with the psalmist in dire distress and with Jesus on the cross 'My God! My God! Why hast Thou forsaken me?'

If I could use those exact words I should be safe, for in spite of feeling absolutely forsaken, I should be crying out in faith, as well as in desperate need, 'My God, still *my* God,' My link with the source of all love and power, though dangerously near to breaking point, would still be holding.

I remember when the two American astronauts who circled the earth visited Australia, one of them was asked by a schoolboy 'Did you find God up there?' The reply was spontaneous and quietly confident 'I found God up there just as much as I find him down here.'

The spirit of God fills the universe, there is nowhere where God is not present. Nothing can keep him out. 'Look, I am with you always, even to the end of time.' 'When you pass through the waters, I will be with you; and through the rivers, they shall not overwhelm you, when you walk through the fire you shall not be burned, and the flame shall not consume you.' (Isaiah 43.2).

A grain of faith, even an imperfect practice of prayer, will reveal the divine presence and enable us to come through, spiritually unscathed. That presence stays with us through death and beyond. Prayer is realising God's omnipresence.

92 Personal Radio

There can be few people who have not felt concerned for a dear one facing a serious operation, or a friend facing some crises in life or an acquaintance involved in some failure in integrity or nerve. Such concern comes very near to prayer and is often expressed in prayer for the healing, strengthening and well-being of those whom we love or for whom we are concerned.

Such prayer is called intercession, which means placing ourselves between them and God, making ourselves a link between their needs and griefs and the love and sustaining grace of God. God has his own direct relationship with them, but our link may be an additional channel, a human one. I think of such prayer as lifting people to God's presence, holding them in his healing X-ray, believing that whatever happens he is with them and all shall be well. Nothing can snatch them out of the Father's hand.

I used to think of intercession as a duty, which I performed spasmodically and with an effort. Then one day a friend suggested I should think of it as the prayer of love, and then it became exciting. Another friend said intercession was like holding up a mirror to the sun so that its rays were reflected to someone in a dark hole. A radio engineer told me that he thought of it as a personal radio which sent out impulses of love reflected down from the over-arching love of God, transmitted and magnified by the divine energy.

Prayer is not limited by space or time, it is immediate and faster than the speed of light. Jean Waddell, who was my secretary for five years in Jerusalem, told me a few days ago that she knew she was being supported by the prayers of many people when imprisoned in Iran.

I know how casual and uncostly my remembrances in prayer can become, and so I am learning slowly to repeat before God a number of times the names of those for whom I ask his blessing. I remember too the prophet Samuel's reply to King Saul's request that he should pray for him: 'God forbid that I should sin against the Lord in ceasing to pray for you'.

93 The tempo of life

In these days we live under the pressure of time: people who commute to their work; mothers of families; drivers of motor cars; journalists who have to keep to a deadline; even busy diocesan bishops. The pressure of time may be a fact, the feeling of haste, sometimes amounting to panic, is psychological, even spiritual. Is it possible to be unhurried within ourselves, however much may be the pressure that comes from without, over which we have little control?

As we read the gospels, we get the impression that Jesus was never hurried, never worried, never muddled, never near to breaking point, because he was in touch with God and so had an interior life that was peaceful.

I find that when I have the sense to take a few minutes quiet when things are in danger of getting on top of me, time seems to slow down. Whereas before things seemed to be coming at me in a frontal attack, after a little quiet with God, I realise that they can come in a queue, so that I give my full attention to each as it comes, without spoiling the first by worrying about the second or third. If in addition to this, I make a practice of a daily time of quiet, when the heart and mind are stilled even from thought, the peace of God enters into the rush and turmoil of daily life. In the spiritual dimension there seems a different kind of time, things sometimes get slowed up, and sometimes there comes a immediacy which deals with the problems at hand.

A text from Isaiah often comes to steady me: 'They that wait upon the Lord shall renew their strength; they shall mount up with wings as eagles; they shall run, and not be weary; they shall walk and not faint' (Isaiah 40.31). When sudden decision and action are needed, they see what to do; when they have to keep going under pressure they are enabled to do so; in the long unexciting stretches of duty, they are kept faithful and patient. The tempo of heaven takes over.

94 Weekly oasis

A few weeks ago I stood once again by the sea of Galilee. It was early morning, the unpredictable lake was quiet and still, not a boat was in sight. The hills on the other side of the lake reminded me of how Jesus often went apart with his disciples to be quiet with God. It is easier to think of him there than in the narrow crowded streets of Jerusalem, with the many groups of pilgrims being hurried round by their guides.

I remembered the hymn of Whittier:

O Sabbath rest by Galilee!
O calm of hills above,
Where Jesus knelt to share with thee
The silence of eternity,
Interpreted by love?

The human spirit needs these periods of quiet — early morning, quiet evening, the silence of the night, or occasional oasis during the day when one withdraws into the quiet of the heart to be refreshed and renewed in the rush and pressure of life.

Whittier's hymn continues:

Drop thy still dews of quietness
Till all our strivings cease
Take from our souls the strain and stress
And let our ordered lives confess
The beauty of thy peace.

I remembered Runciman's paragraph in his History of the Crusades (pub. Cambridge University Press):

The desire to be a pilgrim is deeply rooted in human nature. To stand where those we reverence once stood, to see the very sites where they were born and toiled and died, gives us a feeling of mystic contact with them and is a practical expression of our homage. And if the great men of the world have their shrines to which their admirers come from afar, still more do men flock eagerly to those places where, they believe, the Divine has sanctified the earth.

95 Cares into prayers

Many people seem to think that worry is an expression of virtuous concern. On the contrary it is a subtle sin for it amounts to a distrust of God — his love, his will, his grace. Moreover, it makes one confused in mind and unable to think clearly. We should take any quiet forethought possible, and then trust God to guide and strengthen us to meet each duty, difficulty or emergency, as it comes.

The prophets of the Hebrew Bible were constantly challenging the thinking and behaviour of their contemporaries and the policy of their rulers. This inevitably led to trouble, but they were unafraid for they believed that in speaking out they were doing the will of God, bringing a relevant word from him, pointing out the consequence of wrong ways. 'Thou wilt keep him in perfect peace', says Isaiah, 'whose mind is stayed on thee because he trusts in thee'.

Jesus was never muddled, never worried, never hurried, never on the edge of a nervours breakdown, because his mind was anchored in God. One might think that this was not so in that hour of agony in Gethsemane, but surely the struggle there was to assure himself that death, seemingly the defeat of all his hopes, was God's will and that the issue could be safely left in God's hands. A little later, as a result of his prayer, he was able in calm dignity and with no trace of fear, to hand himself over to those who had come to seize him.

In his earlier teaching, he had urged men not to be anxious, but to trust the heavenly Father who was conscious of their daily needs and problems, and would guide them in his loving wisdom.

'Cast all your cares on him', urges St Peter, 'for he cares about you'. 'Have no anxiety about anything', advises St Paul, 'but in everything by prayer and thanksgiving let your requests be made known to God'. In short, turn cares into prayers.

Yet all the time we must be building an order of society which cares for all in need and makes provision to help them. So we take our part in the advancement of God's kingdom of righteousness.

96 Happy birthday

I sometimes think that the completed person will have undergone four births in the course of his development, each accompanied by a certain amount of travail. The first is our physical birth, when each emerges from the body of the mother in which the fertilized ovum, bearing chromosomes inherited from both parents, has been protected and nourished during the nine hidden months of growth.

The second birth is a psychological one, when eyes begin to focus, limbs to co-ordinate, people are recognised, thought, speech and memory begin to develop, and a relationship with the people around gradually forms, resulting in growth in knowledge and the beginning of self-consciousness and understanding.

The third birth is the spiritual one, what religious people call conversion, enlightenment, *satori*, the recognition of a spiritual constituent, something additional to body and mind, akin to the creator spirit, with whom we may have conscious relationship. Something happens within this spiritual constituent, when we decide to live according to what we know of the God in whose image we believe ourselves to be made.

Saul of Tarsus experienced this on the Damascus road when he cried out: 'Lord, what wilt thou have me to do?' That was his moment of spiritual birth. Sometimes this happens in a moving emotional experience; with some people, however, it happens in a quiet growth, a warming glow, an inner assurance of acceptance and peace. The whole life is put 'under new management'.

The fourth birth is what we usually speak of as death. This is a birth into the spiritual and the eternal. Its birthpangs are often felt in the growing limitations and humiliations of old age, which that saintly thinker, Teilhard de Chardin, spoke of as being hollowed out ready to be filled with the spiritual, a loosening of the physical ties that bind us in the material and temporal. The earthly bugler will hardly have finished sounding the Last Post when the trumpeter on the other side will be sounding Reveillé.

97 Unfinished story

I am sometimes asked why I believe in life after death. My first attempt at an answer is because I believe in God. Having set in motion a process which finally produced man, conscious of himself and for ever seeking the cause of his being I cannot believe that God would cut him off just when he was beginning to be aware of his spiritual nature, potentiality of further growth and conviction of value in the sight of God.

My second attempt at an answer is because Jesus believed in life after death, and I am his disciple because both in his words and life he shows me God. A third reason comes from the experience of his first disciples, who believed that he was still with them after death.

I freely admit to wishful thinking. I want to meet again those I have known and loved, who before they 'died' helped me by their friendship and encouragement. If God is love as Jesus taught, then love is eternal, and a relationship of love cannot be broken by physical death.

I am glad that Jesus died, for in his death he shows his solidarity with us, for we all have to die. Death to the believer in God is not the end of life but the gateway to more life, in a new mode of being independent of time, space and body presence. Death is then our final birth, into the spiritual and the eternal, and the diminishments and humiliations of old age are our hollowing out ready to be filled with eternal life, the breaking of the physical molecules so that they may be transformed into the imperishable.

So I can rejoice with St Paul when he says 'Whether we live we live unto the Lord, and whether we die we die unto the Lord. Whether we live therefore or die, we belong to the Lord, for this cause Christ both died and rose again that he might be Lord both of the dead and the living!'

98 The last enemy?

Everywhere people fear death. It is an uprooting, a rending apart of body and spirit, an adventure into the unknown, leaving behind loved ones, as well as the many beautiful things of earth. No wonder that many think of it in mortal grief and fear. St Paul spoke of it as the last enemy to be destroyed.

Death is the ultimate fate of all of us. Surely therefore it must be part of God's plan for human life, and therefore good. Is it the end of life or the beginning of new and more life? Is it going away from home or going home where we really belong? An American poet has said:

I have seen death too often to believe in death.
It is not an ending, but a withdrawal,
As one who finishes a long journey,
Stills the motor,
Turns off the lights,
Steps from his car
And walks up the path
To the home that awaits him.

St Paul, meditating on the resurrection of Jesus, asks 'Where now, O death, is your power to hurt us? Where now, O grave is the victory you hoped to win?' According to this, the grave is not our final home. It may be that we should not regard death as an enemy at all but think of it, as Jesus did, as going to the Father.

In the acted parable of Lazarus, Jesus says to Martha 'I am the resurrection and the life; he who believes in me, though he die, yet shall he live.' These words are quoted at most Christian funerals, but often intoned so solemnly and sadly as to belie the tremendous meaning they contain. They are a triumphant expression of faith — in life — in the presence of death, with the coffin and the corpse so much the focus of attention.

The deathless quality of the life promised is seen in the life of Jesus, both before and after his physical death. It is pledged in the goodness of God, who, we believe, will not cut off those whom he has brought to being, just as they may be reaching some level of spiritual maturity.

99 Signs of life

There are three resurrection miracles or signs in the gospels, which precede the greatest of all miracles, namely the resurrection of Jesus.

The first is the raising of the little daughter of Jairus, to whose bedside Jesus is called, but seemingly too late. Taking her by the hand, he speaks to her. She hears his voice and is recalled to life. A child a few minutes dead is able to hear and to respond.

The second incident is the raising of the widow's son at Nain. He has been dead for some hours, and the funeral is taking place on the same day. When Jesus calls to him, he is recalled to life. A man whose body is on the way to the cemetery is able to hear the voice of Jesus and to obey.

The third takes us into a longer time interval. Lazarus of Bethany has been dead for four days; his body has begun to decay. Jesus calls to him in a loud voice 'Lazarus, come out!'. The dead man, bound with the clothes of death, comes out of the cave-tomb. A man, four days dead, has heard the voice of Jesus.

All three acted-parables are taken by the evangelists as fulfilment of our Lord's promise 'Truly, truly, I say to you, the hour is coming and now is, when the dead will hear the voice of the Son of God, and those who hear will live'.

On another occasion, as reported in the fourth gospel, Jesus says 'Truly, truly, I say to you, if any one keeps my word, he will never *see* death'. So great will be the divine life within him that he will hardly notice death when it comes. A minute later Jesus says that such a man 'will never *taste* death' he will hardly feel it, but take it in his stride.

The three incidents we have been considering are miracles or signs before our Lord's own resurrection. That was the greatest sign of all, by which the mission of Jesus was established and approved, and the kingdom of heaven thrown open to men of faith, trust and obedience. God's will is that all men of every generation shall enter into it.

100 Eternal moment

The moment when Jesus died must have been a heartbreaking one for his mother, Mary Magdalene and John, to the rest of the twelve, to the Galiliean friends who a few days earlier had cheered him as he entered Jerusalem. It brought two highly placed friends out into the open, Nicodemus and Joseph of Arimathea, who helped to take down his lifeless body. It brought also an unexpected tribute from the Roman soldier in charge of the execution: 'Truly this man was a son of God' (New English Bible). 'This man was a great and good man' *(Jerusalem Bible).* The two disciples going to Emmaus two days later sadly remarked 'We had been hoping that he was the man to liberate Israel'.

With Jesus it was otherwise. His study of the scriptures of his nation had convinced him that he must be ready to die. Only death would convince people of the limitless nature of his own and God's love. His last words proved that his view of death was going to God. If death was God's will, then he could leave the sequel in God's hands. Death would not be the end. In God's time both sequel and meaning would become clear.

I sometimes think that the whole of the next 50 days was gathered into that one moment of Christ's death — death, going to God, resurrection, exaltation, and the release of his loving, eager spirit to become a universal presence, the sending out of the remaining eleven messengers to the whole world and the mission of the Church in every generation. It could have been gathered up in one eternal, timeless moment, though it would take weeks before all that became clear. John in his gospel took only three days to realise its meaning.

What happened to Jesus, the perfect Son of God, is meant to happen to us his brothers and sisters who can now call God Father. The seed has fallen into the earth and died, the seed implanted by God in the heart of every man and woman can germinate and burst into flower. The veil between earth and heaven has been torn from top to bottom, and an endless procession follows Jesus to the presence of the Father.